Y0-EDT-930

SOME WOMEN
OF FRANCE

MADAME DE STAËL

SOME WOMEN OF FRANCE

By

PAUL BARRON WATSON

Essay Index Reprint Series

BOOKS FOR LIBRARIES PRESS
FREEPORT, NEW YORK

First Published 1936
Reprinted 1969

STANDARD BOOK NUMBER:

8369-1433-3

LIBRARY OF CONGRESS CATALOG CARD NUMBER:

73-90691

PRINTED IN THE UNITED STATES OF AMERICA

FOREWORD

✳

THE handful of essays contained in this little volume
has no other purpose than to whet one's appetite for more
elaborate studies. They were compiled merely as a pastime by
a busy lawyer who loves France and admires many of the traits
of French people. There are certain things about the French
which Anglo-Saxons do not readily comprehend. Chief of
these is the extraordinary influence which women have exerted
in almost every period of French history. To some extent
this is due to innate characteristics of the Latin races. They
are people of warm emotions. But the main reason why

v

French women have been able to play a leading part is that
they are carefully educated in those things which in the natural order of events will be the chief preoccupation of their
lives. Appreciation of art and architecture, correct diction,
posture, the art of conversation, social amenities of every kind,
are fundamentals of every French girl's training. Of still
greater importance, every girl, before her schooling is ended,
has an exhaustive knowledge of her country's literature. She
can read, if not speak, English and Italian. And, above all,
she has acquired skill in literary composition. The humblest
seamstress in France can write a letter which reminds one of
madame de Sévigné. Then, too, most French women are distinguished by an intense enthusiasm for their native land.
Beginning with Jeanne d'Arc and running through the days of
the Revolution, when madame Roland was sacrificed on the
scaffold, women have vied with men in deeds of heroic courage. Female heroism stands forth almost as a national cult.
To record the doings of all those women who have added
luster to France would not be possible in a single book. The
women whose lives are herein pictured are no more famous
than many others. Most of them have been chosen for discussion simply because they do not seem to the writer to
have been adequately treated in other works.

CONTENTS

LIST OF ILLUSTRATIONS

SOME WOMEN
OF FRANCE

HÉLOÏSE

✶

THE story of Abélard and Héloïse belongs to a period only two hundred years after the history of the French nation began. There was then no capital of France, the king making his headquarters sometimes at Orléans, sometimes at Compiègne, more rarely at Paris. Louis VII, weak and irresolute, was king. None of the present cathedrals had been begun and there were then no schools. There was no political cohesion of the country, the king's authority being nominal rather than real, some of his vassals having greater power than himself. Paris was little larger in population than some of

1

the other towns, but it was beginning to rise in importance through its cathedral which was soon to be demolished to make place for the present cathedral of Notre-Dame. The only power that was universally acknowledged was the Church, and a mighty power it was because it was only through the Church that men and women could learn to read and write. Outside the Church there was no such thing as books. People, bathed in superstition, flocked to churches and saw robed priests and dignitaries reading from illuminated parchments which seemed to them as mystical as the great edifices of modern times would seem to the wild inhabitants of central Africa. The holders of these ecclesiastical offices, in the eyes of the people, were supermen. All others belonged to a different class of humanity between whom and these mystical supermen existed an almost impenetrable gulf. Abélard, born in 1079, was the first person of prominence to take active measures to build a bridge across this gulf. There is no question that he was influential in at least inspiring people with a zeal to acquire learning outside the sacred precincts. Driven from his priestly duties because of insurrection he used his oratorical gifts to enlighten people who came to hear him lecture; and his boldness in denouncing some of the Church doctrines was the forerunner of a freedom of discussion which four centuries later brought about the Reformation.

✳

OF ALL the love-stories that have come down to us in history or in fiction none has thrilled more hearts than the story of Abélard and Héloïse. For nearly eight hundred years the bodies of these passionate lovers have been cold, but men still visit the cemetery of Père-Lachaise and place their garlands on the famous tomb to prove their admiration for undying love.

To become acquainted with this drama we do not have to rely on hostile critics or on sympathetic friends. It is all unfolded in a bundle of letters that passed between the lovers twenty years after the episode was closed; and it is safe to say no love-story was ever told with greater pathos or with less desire to gloss over the painful incidents of a cruel fate. Those letters have always ranked high as specimens of medieval literature, but they are valuable above all else because they disclose with unrivalled clarity the depth and fulness of a woman's love.

It was no ordinary suitor to whom Héloïse gave her heart. When she first met Abélard he was already a distinguished man. Scion of a well-to-do Breton family, from early youth he had been fired with a zeal for scholarship. Leaving home at fifteen, he had wandered from place to place in search of education. Schools in the modern sense were then unknown. Charlemagne's ideas of kingly responsibility had long been laid aside and the state had abandoned every effort to educate the people. Learning was to be found nowhere except within the Church, and education was deemed a matter with which the public had no concern. Only in the monasteries was there anything to be called a school, and it was to these monasteries that Abélard, in his thirst for knowledge, turned his steps.

According to his own assertion the branch of knowledge which interested him most was dialectics, or the art of disputation. So it was not long before he wended his way to Paris, to the school of Notre-Dame, presided over by Guillaume de Champeaux, who had the reputation of being the greatest dialectician of his time. Soon he became exasperated by the futility of this school, where the main topic of discussion was whether individuals have any existence apart from the mind.

Though little more than a boy he did not hesitate to dissent from the arguments of the learned teacher and to tell him to his face that what he said was "nothing but words." As he might have contemplated, this brought his schooling to a close.

Then he opened a school of his own at Melun where he found many pupils eager to hear his lectures. After a short period he moved to Corbeil just outside of Paris. There his health broke down and he returned to Bretagne to regain his strength.

Coming back to Paris a few years later he found things greatly changed. Guillaume de Champeaux was no longer there, and the chair at Notre-Dame was offered to Abélard. He did not hold it long, however, and after another short sojourn at Melun he opened a school at Sainte-Geneviève on the left bank of the Seine and just across from Paris.

About this time he learned that his father had become a monk and his mother was about to enter a convent. He caught the prevailing craze himself and determined to study theology. With that in view he went to Laon and after a most superficial preparation began to lecture on the Scriptures. This so irritated the clergy at Laon that he returned to Paris and held himself out as a full-fledged lecturer on the doctrines of the Church.

Paris was now becoming a cosmopolitan city where anyone with new ideas was sure to get a hearing. Abélard had already proved himself an original thinker who did not hesitate to attack accepted beliefs, and he was quick to see that as a public lecturer a conflict with those in authority would increase his fame. He therefore took a stand in theological matters which differed somewhat from the ordinary teaching. He did not deny the dogmas of the Church, but he asserted that the Christian faith was to be reached through the intellect and not accepted simply because adopted by the fathers of the Church. Naturally this aroused the ire of the ecclesiastics, but it did not detract from Abélard's reputation as a public speaker.

The fact was, he had caught the ear of the people, and it was not long before he was the idol of Paris. By his eloquence and magnetic power he became the most popular lecturer of his time, and thousands of people flocked each day to listen to his words.

Up to this time he had lived the life of an ascetic. All his hours had been spent in rigorous and exhausting study. As he put it, he had been educated "in the lap of Minerva." An overweening ambition for applause had excluded him from the pursuit of pleasure, and he had never allowed himself to swerve from his resolution to acquire fame as a scholar. All the emotions of youth had been repressed until he reached the pinnacle of his fame, and then they suddenly burst forth in a torrent which could not be stayed.

He was thirty-nine years of age when there appeared among his pupils a young girl of eighteen whose uncle was a canon of Notre-Dame—one of the places where Abélard had lectured. She had been educated with the greatest care and had shown extraordinary aptitude for learning. In

Abélard's words, "In face she was not inferior to other women, and in the abundance of her learning she was supreme." That was his estimate of her penned twenty years later. It is a meager portrait of Héloïse when she first came into Abélard's life. Keen as her intellect was, she was above all else a creature of flesh and blood in whom the outstanding characteristic was a capacity for overwhelming love.

From the moment when she first saw Abélard she was ready to throw herself at his feet. Captivated by his eloquence, and thrilled by the grace of his personality, he seemed to her a god. "Who among kings or philosophers could equal you in fame? What kingdom or city or village did not burn to see you, and who, I ask, did not hasten to gaze upon you with straining eye? What maid or matron did not yearn for you in your absence, or burn when you were present?"

Abélard would have been less than human had he not been flattered by her adulation. He had no thought of marriage. According to accepted practice philosophers and theologians did not take upon themselves the burden of domestic ties. To do so would have caused derision and brought Abélard's success as a debater to a close. But he wanted this fascinating and rapturous woman, and, as he himself admits, was bent on her seduction. That was so customary a proceeding in those days that it would have excited little comment. But Héloïse was under the guardianship of a rigid uncle who never allowed her to escape his watchful eye. One thing the canon desired above all else—to train his niece's mind—

and so, in a moment of unwariness he consented to take Abélard under his roof with the understanding that Héloïse was to
be his pupil. Needless to say, the atmosphere was not conducive to study, and it was not long before Héloïse found herself with child. To escape the uncle's wrath Abélard spirited
her away and left her at his ancestral home in Bretagne where
she gave birth to a boy. Knowing that the situation must
sooner or later be disclosed, Abélard made bold to face the
canon and offered to marry Héloïse on condition that the
marriage be kept secret. By this proposal he expected to avert
the storm. But when he broached the project to Héloïse she
pleaded with him to give it up. Ignoring her own humiliation,
she urged him not to marry, since it might hamper his career.
The burden of a household would distract his thoughts. She
was his to do with as he would, but he must not be weighted
down with the duty of caring for her support. Much as he
would have liked to shirk responsibility, he dared not brook
the canon's wrath. He therefore married her and left her in
her uncle's house.

Apparently Abélard's ardor had now cooled and he cast
about for some method of shaking off the yoke. With heartless disregard of the young girl's preferences he persuaded
her to enter a convent, hoping in that way to regain his freedom. But a dreadful punishment awaited him for his brutality. The canon's friends resolved to have their revenge. One
night while he was sleeping several of them entered his house,
overpowered him, and before leaving they had wreaked their

vengeance on him in a manner that left it in his power no longer to incur the canon's wrath.

To hide his shame Abélard retired to the abbey of Saint-Denis and became a monk.

It was not long before this stormy petrel became involved in controversy with the abbot of Saint-Denis. He was summoned before a council of the Church at Soissons because of a book which he had written on the holy trinity. He was condemned and required to burn the book. Then he embroiled his associates by questioning the authority of their patron saint. This raised such a storm that he was expelled from the abbey.

Betaking himself to Bourgogne he built a little hut in the wilderness about three miles from Nogent-sur-Seine, and began to lecture to the peasants of the neighborhood. The place became famous, and crowds gathered from every direction to hear him talk. His pupils built for him an oratory to which he gave the name of Paraclet—the Comforter—in recognition of its having served as a refuge when he was in distress.

While at the height of his success at Paraclet, the abbot of a monastery in Bretagne died, and the monks elected him to the vacancy. The ecclesiastical authorities of France, wishing to get rid of him, forced him to accept and he reluctantly abandoned Paraclet.

About this time the convent at Argenteuil where for nine years Héloïse had been sequestered was closed and the nuns driven out. This brought Abélard into the limelight once more. He persuaded Héloïse, with some of the other evicted nuns, to go to Paraclet and establish a little convent there. Soon after, he succeeded in having her appointed abbess, and it was at Paraclet that she passed the rest of her days, scarcely ever seen in public, spending virtually all her time in prayer. At first her life in Paraclet involved much hardship, as she was wholly without means to keep the place going. Abélard visited it occasionally until the people of the neighborhood took up the burden of its support. Then he dropped out of sight and ceased even to communicate with Héloïse.

The fact is, Abélard's time was fully occupied in quarrels with the monks of his abbey in Bretagne. The grounds of his conflict with them are not entirely clear. He tells us that the occupants of his abbey were dissolute and were constantly in rebellion against him, at one time going so far as to put poison in his food. Finally existence among them became so unbearable that he gave up charge of the abbey and returned to Paris, where he again took up his profession as a lecturer.

Meanwhile he was constantly engaged in writing on theological topics and getting into controversies with the authorities of the Church. He wrote another book on the trinity for which he was summoned before a council of the Church held at Sens. The judges found his teaching heretical, and he appealed to Rome. On his way thither he stopped at the Benedictine abbey at Cluny. There he was taken ill and could go no farther. In his absence the pope sustained the decree against him. He then went to Chalon-sur-Saône where he died, April 21, 1142, in his sixty-third year.

His had been a tempestuous life, ma᾽ ed by continuous conflict, much of which was due to his disregard for the feelings of those with whom he had to deal. But he was a forceful writer, and his teaching exerted a permanent influence upon the Christianity of his time. His chief book he called Yes and No. It was arranged in three columns. In the first column were one hundred and fifty-eight dogmas of the Church. Against each dogma were extracts from the writings of two Church fathers on that dogma, the views stated in the second and third columns being diametrically opposed. The purpose was, of course, to show that the fathers disagreed, and that we must rely for our interpretation of Church dogma not upon the fathers but upon our own intelligence. That was a bold assertion and amounted almost to heresy in the day when it was written. But to an ordinary layman it seems to be based on common sense, and to-day it is hardly conceivable that anyone would declare him wrong.

When Abélard was in the midst of his troubles in Bretagne, he had written a letter to a friend describing his calamities. That letter fell by chance into the hands of Héloïse, and it caused a flood of memories to surge up in her brain. The evidence of her abandonment was too clear to be open to question. She knew that Abélard would never make an effort to see her again. She had become resigned to that. But there still lingered in her breast the faint hope that some day she would receive a letter telling her that she still had a place in his heart. This letter had never arrived, but in the one to his friend he had mentioned her in terms which, cold as they were, showed that he was not oblivious of the joys of long ago. She could not resist the opportunity to tell him she had read his words and that her feelings toward him had never changed.

Looked at purely from an artistic point of view, the letter with which she began this celebrated correspondence is a literary gem. It was inspired by a single purpose—to fan into new life the embers of a romantic attachment that was virtually dead. No longer was there any thought of sensuality in their love. She hoped only to kindle in Abélard a desire for spiritual communion which would mitigate her loneliness and give her courage to bear the misery of her blighted hopes.

With this in view she begins by telling him what comfort it has brought her to see again his familiar handwriting. "I began the more ardently to read because the writer was so dear to me, gaining refreshment from his words as from a picture of one whose presence I have lost."

She then offers him her sympathy, and denounces in even more bitter terms than he had used the despicable wretches who had made his life so hard.

Then, to let him see that their situations are alike, she alludes to her own misery made doubly poignant by her grief for him.

In writing to console his friend he has paid a debt of friendship, but how much greater a debt he owes to Paraclet of which he was the architect, and to its inmates who are his daughters. It is a tender plant, frail because of the weakness of female nature. He is tending another's vineyard and neglecting his own. "Ponder on what you owe to us. Instead of giving so much thought to the obstinate, consider what you owe to the obedient. Instead of bestowing so much on your enemies, meditate on what you owe to your daughters."

And he owes a debt not only to Paraclet, but above all else to her who has given up everything for him. At his command she has been joined to him in holy wedlock, and at his command she has renounced all worldly pleasures and become a nun. "If I deserve naught from you, all my labor has been in vain. I can expect no reward from God, for I have done nothing for Him. All I have done has been for you. . . . Remember, therefore, what I have done, and pay heed to what you owe to me."

"And so in His name to whom you have dedicated yourself, before God I beseech you, in whatsoever way you can, restore to me your presence, to wit, by writing me some word of comfort, that thus refreshed I may give myself with more alacrity to the service of God."

Héloïse could not have appealed to him in more effective form. Her language was conciliatory and sympathetic. She based her argument on matters which were of interest to him. Her appeal was dignified and positive, though couched in terms of extreme humility. And she was careful to ask him for nothing which he could not readily grant. She did not demand his love, though her adoration breathes through the letter from the beginning to the end.

It is hard to believe that Abélard could have read this letter without remorse. Though his love had long been dead, he knew full well that he had not given it a decent burial. However he might seek to justify the termination of his emotions, there still remained the duty to shield and comfort the woman whom he had made his wife and who had surrendered all she had in obedience to his command. This duty he had already made up his mind to shirk, and his reply to her appeal reveals a studied effort to ignore the subject that was closest to her heart.

He undertook, however, to give a reason for abandoning the convent of which she was the head. With heartless insincerity he tells her she is so endowed with divine grace that she is able without his aid to kindle religious enthusiasm in those who waver in the faith. This he knew was false. She had entered the convent through no love of God but merely to please him, and he was well aware she claimed no interest in religious things. And was he any more genuine when he suggested that she tell him on what subject she desired him to write? He knew she cared not a whit on what subject he wrote if only he showed a little sympathy and recognized the tie by which they had once been bound.

With an egotism that is almost brutal he suggested that prayers be offered for his own well-being. Unwilling to give her even the satisfaction of feeling that he has made a personal appeal to her, he proposes that all the sisters in Paraclet unite their efforts in his behalf.

And could anything be more cruel than his request that when he dies his body be buried at Paraclet? "The sight of my tomb," he says, "will lead our daughters and sisters in Jesus Christ more frequently to offer their prayers for me before the Lord."

Her answer to this cold epistle shows that he had cut her to the quick. Every word in his letter had merely added to her distress. How, she asks, could she be expected to pray if he were dead; all she could do would be to weep. "A heart torn by sorrow can not be calm. There is no place for God when one is overwhelmed with grief. . . . If I lose you, that is the end of all. Why should I prolong a pilgrimage which I can endure only when sustained by you?"

Her bitterest grief, if the truth were known, came from the realization that she was not permeated by the spirit of holiness demanded by her calling. She was leading an unnatural life, as were many other women of her time. It was the age of monasticism, when men of all classes were being driven to monasteries through sheer ennui. Though priests at that period were not forbidden to marry, most of them preferred to become monks simply because there was so little to interest them in domestic life. For many women, therefore, marriage was out of the question, and great numbers of them retired to convents because it was the only thing that they could do. Those who were not buoyed up by religious zeal found the constant observance of pious duties almost unbearable. Novices might perhaps get some relief in occasional lapses, but to an abbess like Héloïse who was expected to be the pattern for all those under her care every lapse from the path of duty caused a laceration of the heart.

The nuns were constantly exposed to the danger of being led into immorality. Under the system then in vogue each convent was under the authority of a monastery and the nuns owed obedience to the monks of the monastery by which they were controlled. Their convent was subject to constant visitation, and it was difficult to avoid temptation when monks clothed with authority visited a convent occupied by women who had taken the vow of chastity under stress of circumstances and with no predilection for holy living. In Abélard's letter to his friend he declares that the priests through their power over the nuns often led them into immoral practices, and in one of his letters to Héloïse he points out the danger of allowing monks to communicate with the nuns except in the presence of others.

Héloïse suffered intense agony on that score. Her adoration of Abélard kept her pure, but she was a woman of vehement emotions, and her long sojourn at Argenteuil, which was suppressed because of the immorality of the occupants, had made her familiar with the danger to which she was exposed. She was in constant dread of the monks who visited her convent, and in one of her letters to Abélard she asks if she must allow them to sit at her table. "Oh! how easy a step to the destruction of the souls of men and women is their dwelling together in one place! But especially at table, where gluttony and drunkenness prevail and wine is drunk with enjoyment, wherein is luxury."

The fact is that despite her earnest effort to adapt herself to the regimen of the cloister she had never been able to free her mind of carnal thoughts. By prayer and fasting she did all she could to wash away her sins, but in the deep silence of the cloister her mind kept wandering back to the voluptuous pleasures of her youth. She knew the life which she was trying to lead was false. "They say that I am chaste and they do not realize that I am a hypocrite. Purity is not a matter of the body but of the soul. I am honored upon the earth, but I have no merit before God who searches the heart and sees clearly in the hidden places."

She could not conceal from herself the truth that she was not really penitent. "Mortification of the body," she writes, "is not penitence so long as the soul retains a love of sin. It is easy to confess one's faults and endure bodily penance. What is hard is to erase from one's soul the regret for having lost unspeakable happiness. Even during the solemnity of divine worship—at the moment when prayer should be most fervent and most pure—sinful images arise so vividly before me that I cannot fix my thoughts on prayer. I weep not for the faults which I have committed, but for those which I commit no longer. And not only what we did but the hours and places, and all the circumstances relating to them, are victoriously engraven on my memory with your image. I live it all over again. I fall into a sort of delirium. The past has gained complete control of my imagination and leaves me in a state of agitation. Even in my sleep I cannot rest. Sensations permeate my being which I have no power to suppress, and words escape my lips which betray the derangement of my heart."

Whether or not she thought so, Héloïse did not really suffer from a derangement of the heart. What impelled her to this frank confession was the necessity for emotional release. Shut up in a nunnery where the thoughts of her associates were expected to be fixed on holy things, there was no one near her with whom she could freely talk. She needed an outlet and so she turned instinctively to the man who had once been her partner in the scenes which her imagination evoked. We are not required to take too literally the description of her sensations. In the monotony of the cloister she had long been feeding upon her memories of the past. They had become a sort of phantasm surging through her brain, and she was thus led to describe as a reality what was perhaps little more than a dream.

Sensuality was not the basis of her love for Abélard. It is true she said in one of her letters that she would rather be his mistress than his wife. To use her own language she "preferred love to matrimony, freedom to a bond." But the reason which she gives for this preference indicates that her thoughts were pure. A wife, she says, is looking for a reward, whereas she wished to give herself without asking for anything in return. Physical union had no meaning to her except as an expression of the communion of souls. During the nine years of her stay at Argenteuil no scandal ever smirched her name, and while she was abbess at Paraclet her life was always decorous. No image but that of Abélard ever touched her heart. It permeated every fiber of her being. She was bone of his bone, flesh of his flesh. It was an unreasoning, unquenchable passion which even his indifference to her was powerless to efface.

In reading these letters one is tempted to question whether Héloïse would not have shown more worldly wisdom had she made some effort to curb the expression of her love. Much of the joy in wooing comes from the ardor of the chase, and the prize is valued often because it is difficult to win. But we must not forget that this correspondence began when the chase had reached its end. There was no longer any need for diplomacy. Her only purpose was to tell Abélard frankly what was in her heart, and she spoke with sincerity when she told him her whole being was wrapped up in him. Abélard had lauded her for her piety, and she replies: "God knows it is your command, not the voice from heaven, that has placed upon me the monastic yoke. Consider my desperation, after all the suffering I have undergone on earth, when I realize that I can have no recompense on high. Until now my dissimulation has deceived you as it has others. You have attributed to religious enthusiasm what was only a sham. In commending yourself to my prayers, you demand the very thing I ask of you.

"Do not, I implore you, place your trust in me, lest you fail to aid me by your prayers. I am not healed; so do not deprive me of the sweetness of the remedy. I am not enriched by grace; so do not delay in succoring my misery. I am not strong; so take care lest I fall before you have come to my relief.

"Therefore, please, a truce to your praise. Do not incur

the shameful reproach of flattery and falsehood with which we charge the poor. If you believe there is yet in me any vestige of virtue, take care that it be not blown away by the breath of vanity. A wise doctor sees the hidden malady though no symptoms betray it.

"I am made too happy by your praise and my heart abandons itself too easily to your flattery. I am too much disposed to be intoxicated by the sweet poison, for my sole study is to please you in everything. Summon your fears, I beg of you, and lay aside your confidence, that your solicitude may ever be ready to help me.

"Do not exhort me to virtue. Do not incite me to combat by telling me virtue reaches its height in weakness, and that the crown will be given only to the one who combats to the end. I seek no crown of victory. All I want is to avoid danger. It is wiser to shun peril than to engage in war. If God will give me but the smallest corner in heaven, I shall be satisfied."

The response which Abélard made to this affecting letter brought some comfort to her troubled heart. While it made clear to her that she could never hope again to kindle his affection, it contained a genuine admission of the wrong that he had done. It attempted to prove to her that the physical affliction which had been visited upon him was a just punishment from God, and was a blessing in that it had deprived him of further opportunity to sin. He exhorts her to forget that she has been his wife and henceforth to think of herself only as the bride of Christ.

If we may judge by her next letter (the last we have from her) his admonition calmed her excited nerves, and whatever her emotions may have been she did not thereafter give them utterance.

To speak the truth, this last letter from her is so different in style and substance from her earlier letters that one is almost tempted to suspect it was not hers. While purporting to ask Abélard to enlighten her on the origin of the institution of nunnery and to prescribe rules for guidance of the sisters in their work, it is itself a treatise on the very subjects on which it craves enlightenment. It seems almost as if it were written by Abélard as a preface to the last two letters from him which close the correspondence. At any rate it furnishes no clue to the outcome of her love. We do not know whether she finally became reconciled to her fate. From other sources we learn that she was still an inmate of the convent when Abélard died. His remains were transferred to Paraclet in compliance with his request, and upon her death twenty-one years later their bodies were united in a single tomb.

ISABEAU de BAVIÈRE

✗

THE three hundred years between the death of Héloïse and the birth of Isabeau entirely changed the face of France. Though little change was effected in the lives of peasants, more and more of them abandoned agriculture and clustered together in the towns. In the days of Isabeau important cities were to be found all over France. Municipal government, with all its financial and social ramifications, had become the chief problem on which men exercised their minds. Paris had become the seat of government and was now embellished with handsome edifices, ecclesiastical and secular. Royal expenditure had increased so fast that taxes were a serious burden, resulting in constant insurrection, especially among the peasants, who had no share in the luxurious life of the capital and no interest in the armies kept on foot to protect the personal prerogatives of the king. In no period of French history was there so little loyalty to the crown. With almost complete indifference the people saw the king of England take possession of the northern part of France. Isabeau sat on the throne unmoved while her husband's land was being dismembered and, though then no longer queen, she lived to see France restored to power through the miraculous courage and enthusiasm of Jeanne d'Arc.

ISABEAU DE BAVIÈRE will never be reckoned among the heroines of France. She has always been called a traitor to the country of which her husband Charles VI was king. The charge against her is that she assented to the treaty by which the king of England was declared the lawful inheritor of the throne of France. That treaty was signed at Troyes on the bank of the Seine in 1420. Because of changed conditions it was not carried out, but Isabeau has never been pardoned for assenting to its terms.

The treaty which caused her to be hated bore no signature but that of Charles, and we look in vain for any evidence that Isabeau attempted to coerce or influence the king. Still, the purport of the transaction was to hand the government over to a foreign power, and Isabeau has had to bear the brunt of calumny simply for the reason that she was not a child of France.

Nothing but reasons of expediency led Charles to seek a wife outside his realm. France, at the time of his marriage, was in the throes of civil war. Five years earlier, at the age of fourteen, he had succeeded to the throne, but the crown was scarce upon his head when his uncles began to quarrel, each resolved to hold the reins. After some bickering it had been determined that the government should be administered by a council of twelve, among whom should be the four uncles of the king. Of these four men the one with greatest influence was the duc de Bourgogne. He was a man of ceaseless energy and of determined will; and he was the only member of the royal family who knew how to govern men. He gradually came, therefore, to take the leading part in governing the country, and it was to him more than to any other that the young king grew into the habit of turning for advice.

By inheritance of his wife the duc de Bourgogne had become possessor of the fertile lands of Flanders, which made it necessary for him to be on terms of amity with the powers of central Europe. His son and daughter had already allied themselves by marriage with the rulers of Bavaria, and he wished to strengthen his position further by negotiating a similar alliance for his protégé the king of France.

It was not altogether easy to bring the thing about. Rich as France was, her affairs were so disorganized that the German princes were not particularly eager to let their daughters go. One of them refused point-blank, and it was only by the persistence of the duchesse de Bourgogne that her husband at last succeeded in carrying the matter through.

In Froissart's Chronicle we are told how Isabeau, the daughter of Étienne, duke of Bavaria, was brought to Amiens and offered to the king. It was apparently a case of love at first sight. "When the damsel was ready, the three duchesses led her to the king, and then she kneeled down; but the king took her by the hands and beheld her well, by which regard love entered into his heart." The next day the ladies conveyed Isabeau "in a chair richly covered, with a crown on her head worth the riches of a realm, which the king had sent to her beforehand; and the bishop of the same place did wed them in the presence of all the lords and ladies."

Isabeau was only fourteen when she became a queen. At her father's simple court she had found no opportunity to become familiar with politics or to study the forces that lie behind men's acts; and she came to the throne having no acquaintance with courtiers or with the difficulties and dangers that beset a monarch's life. Her character was yet unformed and was bound to take its shape from such incidents as might lie across her path.

The stage on which she had to play her part was not conducive to edifying thoughts. All around her were evidences of brutality and corruption. The men and women who hovered about her husband's court were nearly all seeking to gratify their personal ambitions, and some of them were ready to go as far as murder to effect their ends. Even the king's family were at one another's throats. No one seemed to know definitely who was in control. There was inexactness in every detail of administration. Isabeau was expected to conduct her domestic establishment with regal splendor, and yet at times there was not enough revenue to satisfy her simplest wants. No regular system of taxation had been established, and in various parts of the country people would not pay at all. Paris and several of the larger cities were in a state of anarchy. Shops were constantly broken into by marauders, so that the shopkeepers scarcely dared to keep a stock of goods on hand. The country was overrun with soldiers belonging to one faction or another who seized whatever they wanted without even a pretense of paying, and they frequently tore down the peasants' houses to get material for their fires. It seemed as if everyone was animated by selfish purposes and the only arbiter was the sword.

Charles was not much of a comforter during the early years of Isabeau's married life. At this stage of his career he had a mania for warfare and only at rare intervals was he found at home. Under encouragement from the duc de Bourgogne he spent most of his time in Flanders trying to keep the people in subjection. He also made elaborate preparations for invading England, but for one reason or another the expedition never sailed.

All this time Isabeau had been wearing out her youth in keeping up appearances in Paris, at the same time giving birth to children for the king. She resided in Saint-Paul, a palace which the king's father had erected in Paris on the bank of the Seine. Undoubtedly there were moments when she found happiness in the adulation which she received as queen, but her husband's continued absence dimmed her glory, and her physical condition stood in the way of much that she had hoped to do. She was still too young to direct the court alone, and the animosities always breaking out among her husband's relatives were a constant strain upon her nerves.

Four years after her marriage a ray of light was thrown on her troubled existence by the festivity of her coronation. She was only eighteen on that glorious day in June when she made her formal entry into Paris. All the great ladies of the realm were gathered at Saint-Denis to take her hand, and twelve hundred burgesses on horseback were drawn up on both sides of the road over which the procession was to pass. At its head were the king's mother and sister in a closed litter. Then in an open litter came Isabeau. By her side on horseback was the wife of her husband's brother accompanied by the uncles of the king. Next came all the royal duchesses, and these were followed by throngs of titled ladies, some in carriages and others on their steeds.

At the gate of Saint-Denis where the procession entered Paris a spectacle had been prepared to represent a scene in heaven with children dressed as angels chanting hymns. Other scenes were depicted all along the route, and at one place stretched from roof to roof was a rope on which a tight-rope walker performed his antics as the queen rode by. All the houses were aflame with bunting and "there was such people in the streets it seemed as all the world was there."

On reaching Notre-Dame the four dukes assisted the queen and other ladies to alight. The queen entered the church and knelt at the altar. Then the four dukes approached and laid a costly crown upon her head.

From Notre-Dame she proceeded to the Louvre and made her obeisance to the king.

The next day she was anointed by the archbishop in Sainte-Chapelle, and this was followed by a bountiful repast in the palace at which more than five hundred ladies sat down. After that the queen departed in the company of the duchesses and went to the palace of Saint-Paul where the king joined her later in the day.

A still more pleasing ceremony awaited her on the morrow. Scarcely was she awake when forty burgesses of Paris came to her palace bringing a litter filled with jewels. Soon after, two more litters arrived with more presents for the king, the queen, and her sister-in-law. These presents cost altogether more than three thousand crowns in gold.

For a short time now it looked as if there was much happiness in store for Isabeau. Her husband apparently was surfeited with war. He returned to Paris and took a more active part in the government of his realm. The result was that the duc de Bourgogne lost much of his prestige, his counsel was often brushed aside, and in several important matters the king proceeded in direct opposition to his advice. Charles was no longer the pliant youth that he had been before his marriage. He became self-willed and would brook no interference with his plans. Those who were closest began to detect in him an almost insane desire to have his way. The slightest differences of opinion threw him into a rage, and he gradually became obsessed with the idea that those about him had designs upon his life.

When only twenty-four he became embittered by some trivial act committed by the duc de Bretagne and resolved to march against him with his troops. The members of his council implored him to be calm, but he was determined on revenge; and all his uncles and his brother were forced to accompany him with their men. As he neared the town of le Mans he was stricken with fever, and was again urged to abandon the expedition. After a few days he was better and renewed the order to proceed. It was a scorching day in summer and he began to feel exhausted. Suddenly, hearing behind him a spear clashing against one of his men's armor, he imagined that someone was about to attack him. Wheeling round, he dashed into the midst of his followers, slashing right and left with his sword. Finally he was pinioned and it was found that he had lost his mind. He was unable to recognize anyone. He had to be brought back to Creil in the care of his physicians.

The king being now incapacitated, the duc de Bourgogne again assumed control. His wife had become the confidante of Isabeau, and it was said that nobody could speak to the queen except through her.

By careful nursing, the king's mind gradually cleared, and he expressed a wish to see the queen. She had not been told of his illness because she was about to be confined, but as soon as the word was brought to her she hurried to his bedside and her presence seemed to do him good. After some months he had apparently become cured and he returned to Paris. The physicians told her she must provide him with constant diversion, and, though she was about to give birth to her sixth child, she did not spare herself in furnishing all sorts of social entertainment at Saint-Paul. Among these entertainments was a costume ball for one of the ladies-in-waiting who was about to be married. The king and five of his guests were made up with long shaggy hair to represent savages. In the course of the festivities the hair caught fire and two of the men were burned to death. The king himself was badly scorched. The queen fainted and had to be carried to her room.

The next year the king had another attack which lasted

eight months, and from this time till the end of his life, nearly thirty years later, he was subject to fits of insanity which worked havoc with Isabeau's domestic life. In his intervals of sanity he attempted to administer affairs, but so long as he lived Isabeau was kept in a constant state of anxiety and fear. And the most distressing feature was that when his malady came on he was seized with a dreadful horror of his wife. He imagined she was dogging his steps and trying to cause him bodily harm.

A new source of trouble now hovered over the distracted realm. The incapacity of the king had brought into prominence his only brother Louis who was six years younger than the king. In case of the king's death without male heirs he would have succeeded to the throne, and he resented the domination of his uncle. At the time of his brother's first attack he was only twenty, but during the successive maladies of his brother he became the most formidable rival of the duke. He was an exceedingly fascinating youth, strong and athletic, a fluent talker, and with all this he had a taste for literature and art. Unfortunately he was a lavish spender and somewhat dissipated. Between him and the king there was always a bond of deep affection. On one occasion, before Charles lost his mind, they were together in the south of France and the king made a wager of five thousand francs that he could beat Louis riding on horseback to Paris. Louis won, making the journey in four and a quarter days. Shortly after that Charles conferred on him the title of duc d' Orléans instead of duc de Touraine, the title which he had hitherto borne. This may have acted as a spur to his ambition. At any rate he and the duc de Bourgogne were always quarrelling, and it was only through the efforts of Isabeau that they were prevented from drawing swords.

In 1403 the duc de Bourgogne was forced by failing health to yield control, and with the acquiescence of the king the sovereign power was conferred on Isabeau. In the following year, on the death of the duc de Bourgogne, his son endeavored to gain ascendancy at court, and actual war broke out between the houses of Bourgogne and Orléans. Isabeau, though eager to appease both parties, favored the house of Orléans.

It has always been charged against Isabeau that her alliance with Louis was due to infatuation rather than a desire to promote the interests of France. Even while the reins were held by the duc de Bourgogne there had been rumors of improper relations between Louis and the queen; and in 1403, when her eleventh child, Charles VII, was born, people had questioned whether he was really the offspring of the king. How the rumor started is not entirely clear. There is no evidence that the king's suspicions ever were aroused. She appears to have been genuinely devoted to the king and in his lucid moments so was he to her. It seems probable that Louis' wife was the author of the charge. Her husband's gallantries were on all men's lips and were a constant source of irritation to his spouse. In discussing their private matters Isabeau always took the side of Louis and finally excluded his duchess from the court, but the records do not indicate the grounds which actuated Isabeau in taking so radical a step.

It was matter of common gossip that Louis was often seen in the company of the queen, but that is hardly enough to justify complaint. In the absence of the king his brother naturally took his place at court and participated in many of the entertainments given by the queen. That they were kindred spirits there can be no doubt. Both of them loved society and were eager for display. His vivacity and enthusiasm were always comforting, and she generally turned to him when her husband's malady was at its worst. He was with her on November 23, 1407, when she gave birth to her twelfth child, and on the same day when he was returning to his home he was assassinated by an emissary of the duc de Bourgogne.

Isabeau, it is true, was no longer the ingenuous young woman who had kneeled at her husband's feet at Amiens. She had seen much of the disorders of a dissolute court. According to Froissart, the king's malady was the result of riotous living, and it has been hinted that Isabeau participated freely in the revelry that prevailed about her. But if she were guilty of infidelity to her husband it is hard to understand why she and Charles did not become estranged. Except when he was under restraint his wife was always at his side, and in every situation where a difference of opinion was possible she was a stanch supporter of his views.

The assassination of Louis brought terror into the heart of

Isabeau. Her intimacy with him had been so close that she thought it more than likely the next blow would fall on her. Seized with panic she shut herself up in Saint-Paul and a few days later fled with all her children to Melun. The king was then in the midst of a prolonged period of insanity so that it was useless to look to him for help.

The house of Bourgogne was now in full control, and the people of Paris were generally on its side. The Orléans faction had approached the king of England and promised him the duchy of Normandie if he would help their cause. When this treacherous proceeding became known the people were frantic with indignation, and the duc de Bourgogne used it to mollify the king. He admitted that he was responsible for the murder and declared that Louis had been treating with foreign powers in order to get rid of Charles. The poor old king was so muddled that he did not know what to do. Finally he pardoned the duc de Bourgogne and the royal family returned to Paris. This, however, afforded Isabeau no relief. The capital was in such a state of turmoil that no one's life was safe. As a temporary refuge the king took up his abode in Tours. When he came back a mob stormed the palace of Saint-Paul and in the presence of the queen seized a number of her ladies-in-waiting and threw them into prison. The duc de Bourgogne tried to appease them, but without avail. Finding he was helpless he abandoned the government and left Isabeau and her husband at the mercy of the mob. The Orléanist faction then entered the city and assumed control.

Meantime another storm was brewing on the horizon. For

nearly a hundred years the people of England had gazed with covetous eyes on France. In 1346 Edward III had crossed the channel and defeated the French at Crécy. In the following year he had taken possession of Calais and the English had held that city ever since. No further penetration had been possible, but the people of England had never wearied in asserting that Edward through his mother was the grandson of the French king and therefore the throne of France was theirs. In 1413 Henry V, who was the great-grandson of Edward III, became king of England, and he determined to assert his claim.

Conditions in France were such as to give him every reason to expect that he would win. The nation was divided into two camps, each of which in turn had sought his predecessor's aid. Though neither was wholly ready to admit his claim, he knew their animosity for each other would prevent them from uniting their forces to resist. In 1414 he made a formal demand on Charles, and, to soften the asperity of his demand, he offered to marry the French king's daughter Catherine. To this plan Charles, then king in little more than name, gave his assent; but it became soon manifest that he had no power to install the English king. So Henry determined to seize the throne by force. With thirty thousand men he landed in the neighborhood of le Havre. His plan of campaign was to march first to Calais and subjugate the country as he went along. Meantime the council of Charles endeavored to raise an army to resist and appealed to the adherents both of Bourgogne and of Orléans to join in the defense. The duc de Bourgogne replied that he would come, but his armies never took the field. Then came the battle of Agincourt where the French were beaten though they outnumbered the English three or four to one.

The new duc d'Orléans having been taken prisoner by the English, his father-in-law took control of things in Paris and banished the queen to Tours, where she was kept under guard and not even permitted to communicate with her husband. The poor mad king was treated as a nonentity and was virtually a prisoner in the hands of the Orléanists. All of his sons were dead but Charles, a boy of twelve. The duc de Bourgogne, finding it impossible to gain a foothold in Paris, turned to Henry and formed a pact by which he agreed, so long as Henry's campaign lasted, to continue his warfare against the Orléanists whom he called "the enemies of France." The Orléans faction now came out boldly for the dauphin while the duc de Bourgogne held himself before the people as the champion of the queen. In 1417 he went to Tours and persuaded Isabeau to go with him to Troyes where he had established his headquarters. As Charles had appointed Isabeau to act as regent, the duc de Bourgogne was now in position to declare that he was seeking to restore the throne of France. While the unselfishness of his purpose may well be questioned, it is certain that as things then stood his position was more tenable than that of his opponents. The dauphin had no rights so long as Charles still lived, and the people were not yet ready to depose the king. The Orléanists had done nothing to restore order in the capital. Business was at a standstill, and the people were on the verge of starvation. It was manifest that the Orléanists could not establish a stable government or furnish protection to human life. The people were growing every day more discontented and soon they rose in rebellion against the party in control. Right and left the Orléanists were massacred. Those who survived fled from the capital, taking the dauphin with them. The queen and the duc de Bourgogne sent emissaries to Paris in an effort to restore order, and finally, in the summer of 1418, they came themselves. This time they were received with enthusiasm by the people. In the name of the queen a new government was organized and the insurrection in Paris was brought to a close.

While these events were occurring in Paris, Henry was extending his sway in Normandie. One after another of the cities in that populous region had fallen into his hands. Nowhere had he met with organized resistance. Here and there a haughty nobleman had refused to yield, but nearly everybody had accepted what seemed inevitable and a considerable number had gone so far as to join the army of the invader. Rouen, scarcely inferior in size to Paris, still held out, and Henry realized that because of its fortifications it would be exceedingly difficult to take it by storm. He decided, therefore, to surround the city with his troops, and wait till famine forced the inhabitants to capitulate. Six months later, in January, 1419, Rouen surrendered.

With the fall of Rouen the Orléanists virtually withdrew from the north of France. The dauphin, then sixteen, retired to Tours and left to the duc de Bourgogne the task of combating the invader. This was a task which it would have been futile for him to undertake. Henry had shown himself the most capable general of his time. Normandie, already within his grasp, was fast becoming reconciled to his humane administration and was furnishing generous supplies of ammunition and of men. To attack him single-handed would have been the height of folly, so the duc de Bourgogne opened negotiations in the hope of bringing about a truce. A conference was arranged to be held between the two kings, and Isabeau was to be present with her daughter Catherine, as well as the duc de Bourgogne and the duc de Bretagne. When the day for the conference arrived, all were present except Charles, who was too ill to come. Henry was offered Normandie if he would renounce his claim upon the rest of France. This he indignantly refused, and the conference broke up.

At this moment ambassadors arrived from the dauphin to urge a reconciliation between him and the duc de Bourgogne. In the absence of the dauphin it was difficult to arrange details. So it was agreed that he and the duc de Bourgogne should meet a month later and discuss the matter face to face. In the interval Charles was taken to Bourgogne's headquarters and Henry continued his advance toward Paris.

The meeting between the dauphin and Bourgogne bore all the semblance of a duel, only a few friends of the principals being present. The dauphin began by upbraiding Bourgogne for failure to keep his engagements. Bourgogne denied the

charge. In a few minutes both parties had their hands upon
their swords. The dauphin's friends finally prevailed upon
him to withdraw and, while the conference was breaking up,
someone ran a sword through Bourgogne and he died upon
the spot. In the confusion no one was able to say who committed the murder. The dauphin denied having a part in it,
and attempted to renew negotiations; but he found the people
of Bourgogne in no mood for further parley. The murder
had aroused such passions that there was no longer hope of
presenting a united front against the invader. The people of
Paris were at fever heat and were clamoring for an alliance
with Henry who was already at their gates.

At this juncture the new duc de Bourgogne was hardly
free to choose. Public sentiment had undergone a change. In
the capital and in all the north of France the people had
grown so wearied with civil warfare that they were eager to
welcome anyone who could bring order out of chaos, and at
the moment no one was in position to restore order but the
English king. Even the people of Bourgogne were for him
because they believed he would avenge their murdered duke.
Ambassadors were sent to Rouen, therefore, to discuss the
situation, and finally it was agreed that Henry should come
to Troyes and make a treaty with poor old Charles.

On the twenty-first of May, 1420, the treaty was signed at
Troyes. Looking at it with unprejudiced eyes, it was not altogether humiliating to loyal citizens of France. Henry was
not received as king, he was merely declared to be the lawful heir upon the death of Charles. He was to marry the

French king's daughter, and her children were to inherit the crown upon their father's death. Thus both Henry's title and that of his offspring were to be traced through females according to the English law and contrary to the principle hitherto upheld in France. But that the principle was not particularly sacred is manifest when we recall that later Henry IV inherited through the female branch.

The treaty provided also that as soon as Henry became king Normandie should be restored to the crown of France, and Henry should not style himself king of France, as he had hitherto done, until the death of Charles.

To make the treaty more palatable in France there were inserted in it words by which Charles declared, "Since Henry has become my son and the son of our dear beloved queen, we shall honor him and be to him as father and mother." Charles was to hold the crown and all the royal revenues so long as he should live, but the king of England was to govern, acting in concert with the duc de Bourgogne.

In this treaty, signed by Charles, the dauphin was pronounced guilty of horrible crimes, on account of which his father declared no peace should ever be made with him. He had in mind undoubtedly the murder of the duc de Bourgogne, though the king's ire was kindled also by the looting of Saint-Paul while Isabeau was in banishment at Tours, an outrage in which the dauphin seems to have taken part.

Isabeau's share in these negotiations seems to have been confined to seeing that her daughter became Henry's wife. On the face of the treaty it was entirely the work of Charles.

It was not even signed by Henry, a singular omission which is an indication of the desperate condition of France. Henry was in a position where he could command and did not feel the necessity of giving anything in return.

Three months later Henry married Catherine, and the two kings with their queens and the duc de Bourgogne and the duke of Bavaria went to Melun which Henry was holding under siege. After that, Charles and Isabeau retired to Saint-Paul and their public life was at an end. Two years later the great Henry died, leaving a son by Catherine, and in less than three months after the death of Henry poor old Charles died, too. Isabeau sank into oblivion, living in penury at Saint-Paul. Then Jeanne d'Arc, inspired by God, appeared upon the scene, and finally all vestiges of the treaty of Troyes were swept away.

One thing may certainly be said in praise of Isabeau. In spite of all the distress brought on her by her husband's malady, she remained with her husband to the close, and they stood together in opposing what they regarded as the machinations of their son. As things turned out the penalty fell on her. For thirteen years after her husband's death she lingered on, ignored by the ruling power, and died in her palace of Saint-Paul, which had been the center of the nation's festivities while Charles VI was king.

It was a sad life, this life of Isabeau's. Tied to a mad husband to whom she bore twelve children, deserted by her only surviving son, clothed with the garb of royalty and bearing the title of regent, but harassed by lack of means to support the prerogatives of a queen, tossed about by warring factions, threatened by mobs and murderers, held up to execration for acts which she performed at the dictation of others, she dragged out a miserable existence long after all her influence was gone. Finally she was reduced to poverty; and, though mother of the king of France and grandmother of the king of England, her existence was virtually forgotten and she went to her grave unhonored and unloved.

MADAME du DEFFAND

THREE more centuries have slipped away, and we have passed the period of France's greatest power. Le grand siècle is over. Louis XIV has just been laid away and France has not yet come to realize that its era of world supremacy has reached its end. People were still dazzled by the effulgence of the roi soleil. It was the spendthrift age, when society was being supported by the rapidly-diminishing revenues of the state. With mounting deficits wise men foresaw the inevitable crash, but it was the fashion to avert one's eyes. "Eat, drink, and be merry" was the motto of the day. Down in the lower strata of society there was going on a rumbling discussion of the people's rights, but those in power gave no heed; they knew that something radical must happen, but hoped it would be deferred till their own eyes were closed. Madame du Deffand was typical of her times. It was one of her fundamental principles to give no thought to the morrow, but to make each day provide her with such comfort as it could. Happily for her the crash did not come until she was in her grave.

ONE of the ways in which the leaders of French society in the eighteenth century sought to banish ennui was to compose pen-pictures of one another in which they sometimes ventured, under the license which portrait painters claim, to depict more bluntly than would be tolerated in ordinary conversation the foibles and idiosyncrasies of the person to whom the pen-portrait was addressed. When she was seventy-

MADAME DU DEFFAND

seven the marquise du Deffand painted this portrait of herself: "People give madame du Deffand credit for more intelligence than she has. They praise her and they fear her, in both cases without justice. Of intellect and of beauty she has only what came to her by inheritance—nothing unusual and nothing distinguished. Of education she has none. All the wisdom she has was gained by experience. It came late, and only after many bitter experiences."

This picture, though it describes with accuracy what madame du Deffand considered the salient features of her character, makes no mention of those traits which shaped her whole career and caused her to stand out as one of the most interesting figures in the social life of Paris during the fifty years that preceded the Revolution. As she intimates, she was not an intellectual leader, and she was not a famous beauty; but her sound judgment, the brilliancy of her conversation, the warmth of her emotions, and her amazing vitality drew into her salon all the most fashionable men and women of Paris, and enabled her to gain the reputation of being the most celebrated hostess of her time.

When she said that people feared as well as praised her, she was alluding to a trait which more than any other has been caught up by hostile critics, and has led to a wholly erroneous judgment of her character. There is no question that she had a caustic tongue. She herself admits that she often spoke impetuously. But the virtue on which she prided herself above all else was her sincerity, and it is simply because she was sincere and described the motives of those

about her without fear or favor that her letters reveal with
surprising veracity the characteristics of the artificial society
in which she lived.

One of the strange things about madame du Deffand is
that the first fifty years of her life are virtually a blank. She
seldom refers to her early days, and there seems to have been
a tacit understanding among her friends that there was to be
no mention of her past. She tells us more than once that she
has suffered much, but as to the cause of her unhappiness
her lips were always sealed.

In the absence of evidence, it may be permissible to sur-
mise. When she came to Paris from her home in Bourgogne
she found society completely given over to pleasure. It was
the period of the Regency—the most dissolute period in all
French history. Men—and women, too—had no thought of
anything but revelry. Feasting and card playing, and riotous
orgies that lasted all night long, were the main pursuits of
everyone in high position. Marital fidelity, one might almost
say, did not exist. All administrative functions were conducted by titled persons who held their office through inheritance or as a transmissible right acquired through personal
favor of the king. Deffand through the influence of potent
relatives was launched upon this sea of corruption at the age
of eighteen. Possessing no ancestral wealth, her only way to
prevent being submerged was to swim along with the tide and
fascinate those in power by the gifts of personal charm and
intellectual vivacity with which she was richly endowed.
There are on record descriptions of a few riotous entertain-

ments in which we find her name. We know also that she was an intimate friend of one of the most notorious beauties that enjoyed the privileges of the court, and one of her warmest admirers in her later years declared in an unguarded moment that she had been for a short time the regent's favorite. Apart from these scanty references about her early years we are left wholly in the dark, but it is doubtless the incidents of this period that she had in mind when she declared it was through bitter experience that she acquired the wisdom that guided her later life.

When twenty-two she married the marquis du Deffand, a colonel of dragoons, but apparently he was her husband in little more than name. Soon after her marriage she was granted by the regent an annual pension of six thousand francs. This was too much for the irate husband to endure, and he left her—a catastrophe which seems to have caused her little pain. The truth is, she had other admirers to console her for her loss. After a decent pause the marquis returned to her household, but only for a brief period, and thereafter the rupture was complete. Her life after she parted from her husband was that of most of the women of her time, no better and no worse. That she was a social favorite goes without saying, but everything indicates that her thoughts were bent on getting ahead in the world rather than merely chasing after elusive pleasures.

At about this stage in her career madame du Deffand established an intimacy with one of the most illustrious dames of France. At Sceaux, about seven miles to the south of Paris, lived the celebrated duchesse de Maine whose grandfather was the great Condé and whose husband was the legitimized son of Louis XIV and madame de Montespan. Her château was maintained on a scale of almost regal splendor, and, though her intellectual gifts were somewhat below the average, her greatest ambition was to make her home the gathering-place of all the brilliant men and women of her day. Among those whose companionship she most eagerly sought was the gay young Deffand who had dazzled the regent's court with her sallies of wit and humor. Deffand was bored by the inanity of her hostess but dared not refuse the great lady's invitations, and for many years was a constant visitor, sometimes staying for months at a time under the shadow of the dismal duchesse who once remarked that she never was able to rid herself of the things she didn't care for.

Looked at in a worldly aspect Deffand's sojourns at Sceaux marked an important epoch in her life. It was here that she first met Voltaire, with whom she began a spirited correspondence that extended over a period of fifty years, and at Sceaux she became acquainted with Hénault who provided the means that enabled her to establish her Paris salon.

She could not have found a better protector. When her liaison with him began, Hénault held the honorable post of president of the first chambre d'enquêtes. He was then forty-five, twelve years her senior, and he had become somewhat satiated with the gallantries of his youth. No man in Paris had more friends and his urbanity drew all the most desirable persons to his home. He prided himself on his literary attainments which were sufficient to procure for him a seat in the Académie, though it must be admitted that those most capable of judging did not rank his literary productions quite so high as he would have wished. It was Deffand's quick mentality rather than her feminine graces that aroused his interest, and during their forty years of quasi-matrimonial relations he rarely exerted himself to make a conquest of her heart. On both sides it was admitted to be a liaison of convenience. He told her frankly that she was a necessary evil, and she on her side took pains not to be exacting. "You have the key of the fields," she wrote him, "and you need have no fear that I shall ever ask you to give it back to me." After they had known each other some years he was given the much coveted position of superintendent of the queen's household. This post kept him much of the time away from Paris, but made no serious change in their friendship. She wrote to him at one time, "Your letters are my daily bread," and when he came to Paris he was nearly always to be found in the salon which she had established in what had formerly been the convent of Saint-Joseph. Her apartment had formerly been the home of madame de Montespan.

In 1752 a dreadful calamity overtook her—she was becoming blind. To one whose life had been so buoyant it was a terrific blow. Her first thought was that she must escape from the world. With that thought uppermost in her mind, she gave up her home in Paris and returned to Bourgogne.

There she met a young lady by the name of Julie de
Lespinasse who was the illegitimate sister of her brother's
second wife. The poor girl's putative father lived in Lyon,
and when she was four she was taken charge of by her sister;
and as she grew up was employed as governess of her sister's
children. Her illegitimate birth was fairly well known in the
neighborhood, a fact which made her position most humiliating; and her sister did nothing to make it less so. She was
in bitter grief when Deffand became acquainted with her
and was seriously thinking of going into a nunnery. Deffand
took a fancy to her and wanted to help, but she knew her
brother would be indignant if she took her away, as he
feared that if the girl got out of his power the story of her
birth would become more widely known and reflect discredit
upon his wife's family.

In the summer of 1753 Deffand, finding she could not shake
off her eagerness for society, returned to Paris and reopened
her salon in Saint-Joseph's, and about the same time she wrote
to Lespinasse and asked her if she would like to come to Paris
and serve Deffand in the capacity of companion. The young
lady was overjoyed, but expressed a fear that she might be
unhappy in the great world. Deffand replied that Lespinasse
must examine her feelings carefully and be sure that she would
not regret her decision. She writes her, "If you come I will not
announce your arrival. To the people who see you I shall say
that you are a young lady of my province who intends to enter
a convent, and that I have offered you lodgings while you are
finding what you want. After four or five months we shall

both know how we get along with each other." "However," she adds, "the least artifice and the slightest insincerity which you should show in your relations with me would be unbearable. I am by nature distrustful, and if I detect any finesse in those with whom I deal I lose all confidence in them." A few days later she wrote to Lespinasse not to think of coming "if you have not perfectly forgotten who you are, and if you have not firmly resolved never to think of changing your estate." In spite of these precautions Lespinasse came, and shortly after, in the first letter that we have from her, she says, "If you can appreciate all your absence costs me, it would be, if not a second baptism, at least a second agony. It is singular, but nevertheless true, that one of the happiest moments of my life is this agony, since it gives me the opportunity to convince you of the tenderness and sincerity of my attachment." Whether or not these words gave voice to genuine feeling, Deffand accepted them as real, and for ten years Lespinasse remained in her service not only as a companion but as a trusted friend.

Deffand was now totally blind. Sad as that catastrophe was for her it has resulted in inestimable benefit to posterity, for it led to her devoting a large part of her life to correspondence with her absent friends. The letters which she wrote and those which she received are contained in five large volumes, and are almost a perfect mirror of eighteenth-century society. To one who reads between the lines it is easy to trace the causes that were pushing France onward into the Revolution. The struggle for personal advancement, the venality of public officials, the indifference of those in power to the needs of the common people, could not continue without bringing the government to an end. Deffand saw it with her sightless eyes. She proffered, it is true, no remedy, but in that she was surely much less to be blamed than those who were able to see what was going on around them.

What gives these letters their greatest charm is their aptness in delineating character, particularly her own. She had the reputation of being an extraordinary judge of people. Her inability to see the faces of those about her did not lessen, in fact it may have increased, her power to estimate the motives that governed people's deeds. She had a genius for detecting the weak spot in one's armor. And she did not always spare her friends. In saying that people feared her she spoke with perfect truth; and they feared her most because she was nearly always right. One who knew her better perhaps than anyone else has put on record a statement that she interested herself in everything and he had never found her in the wrong.

When she opened her salon for the second time she had reached the age of fifty-seven. The frivolities of her youth had come to an end. It was in that year that her protector Hénault was made superintendent of the queen's household. Though he still continued when in Paris to frequent her salon, his duties at the court deprived her of the glamour of his daily presence. She was forced to find new votaries to hover around her chair. D'Alembert, whom Hénault had picked up in the gutter and who had now become a famous scholar, still clung to her with undiminished admiration. So did Formont, a brilliant dilettante, who she once said was her dearest friend; and so did Pont-de-Veyle, a lifelong admirer who amused everyone by his eccentricities and humor. But such a triumvirate was no basis for the establishment of a fashionable salon; and so the erstwhile favorite of the gay set began to spread her net to draw into her circle the fashionable ladies who she knew were needed to give luster to her social aspirations.

Her aunt the duchesse de Luynes was a lady-in-waiting and is believed to have used her influence in securing for Hénault his post of authority with the queen; but she was a rather austere personage who looked a little askance upon her vivacious niece. The social leader who did more than any other to build up Deffand's salon was the maréchale de Luxembourg. They had long been on terms of intimacy, and in their earlier years had both been participants in the frivolities of their time. The maréchale possessed great wealth and exalted position, and, what was more important, shared Deffand's craving for social intercourse. Through her Deffand was able to fill her modest apartment at Saint-Joseph's with the cream of the aristocracy. The maréchale de Mirepoix, who had a place at court, the princesse de Beauvau, madame de Falcalquier, and later the duchesse de Choiseul, whose husband was at the head of the government, became almost daily visitors at her home.

Under such auspices it was not strange that Deffand's salon became more famous than all the other salons of her time, nor that it should have given the hostess confidence in her capacity to direct the flow of contemporary thought. She had already established a regular correspondence with Voltaire, whom all acknowledged to be the most talented writer of his day, and her house became a rendezvous of those who longed to regale themselves with the latest exhibitions of his scintillating wit. In this correspondence, which lasted almost till Voltaire's death, Deffand developed a literary style which brought into play her extraordinary adroitness in pressing her arguments under the cloak of cajolery. The flippant egotist of Fernay never suspected that she was laughing in her sleeve, and he continued to amuse her guests in the belief that he was dazzling them by his wisdom long after his brilliant correspondent had become aware that his vaunted cleverness was a sham.

For ten years after the reopening of her salon Deffand dominated the social life of Paris. Her only rival at this period was madame Geoffrin, the rich and popular daughter of the bourgeoisie who used to boast that she had never learned to write. Deffand's modest resources did not permit her to compete with the lavish entertainments that drew impoverished geniuses to the house of Geoffrin, but aristocrats were always eager to escape from the sumptuousness of their own establishments and put up with the simple fare of the cultured and witty hostess who presided at Saint-Joseph's.

In neither of the rival salons was there much to remind one of Rambouillet. Gone was the splendor of the olden days when famous scholars were summoned to read their poems to the leaders of society. Stateliness and ceremonial no longer characterized the Paris salon. The court had taken up its abode at Versailles, and Parisian society was given over to elements that were fast becoming inimical to the king. It is significant of the change in social life that Deffand never seems to have alluded to her salon. According to her conception it was not a drawing-room—it was a supper-room to which her friends were bidden every Wednesday and Friday night. At these gatherings the distinguished maréchale de Luxembourg was always the drawing card. The maréchale de Mirepoix and the princesse de Beauvau also lent the luster of their presence, though the astute hostess took care to have them invited on different evenings, lest they scratch out each other's eyes. D'Alembert could always be counted on to amuse the famous ladies by his brilliant sallies, and Pont-de-Veyle, though often taciturn, never failed to come at Deffand's call. Hénault, when in Paris, sat at his lady's side and kept her cognizant of all that was going on. Sometimes as many as twenty-four sat down at her board. They generally arrived at eleven and often lingered half way through the night. Some of them busied themselves with cards, but Deffand, drawing to the fire her chair, or tonneau as she called it, kept up a steady stream of conversation till the last guest had gone.

What could she have found to talk about all these years without ever seeing the light of day? Nothing but her extraor-dinary skill in the art of conversation could have kept her guests awake. It was an age when polite society had no vital interest in anything. Everybody was conscious of the emptiness of existence. They were all living on the surface, afraid apparently to go into anything deeply. It was this dread of penetrating into the serious things of life that drove people to develop the art of talking. Modes of expression took the place of realities. People vied with each other in speaking cleverly about nothing. Witticism was ranked much higher than erudition. Deffand illustrates this tendency as well as almost any other person of her time. She was much given to saying clever things. When cardinal de Polignac told her the story of Saint-Denis whose head was cut off at Montmartre and who picked it up and carried it six miles to its final resting place, she remarked, "Oh, sir, in a case like that it is only the first step that counts." At another occasion she said, "Supper is one of the four main purposes of life; what the other three are I can't remember."

In the intervals between her supper parties Deffand was indefatigable in the cultivation of her friends. If they were accessible, scarce a day passed when she did not sup with one of them. With those who were absent she kept up an almost daily correspondence. Owing to her infirmity she did not regulate her life like other people. Day and night to her were one. Often she did not retire until four o'clock in the morning. Then she would lie abed and breakfast while others were getting up from lunch. Her afternoons were spent in dictating letters or in listening to the reading of some book. Dinner, if she needed one, was served at six, and then she was ready for any sort of excitement that the night might offer.

The fact was she found life a dreadful bore, and all her social glory meant nothing to her but a relief from ennui. It was not so much the vacuity of her intellectual life as the consciousness that she lacked real friends. She was a creature of vehement emotions. Though she had left behind her the passion of youth, her craving for unselfish devotion was as keen as ever, and every day brought her evidence that what she craved was getting farther from her. Hénault's attachment, which had never been deep, was gradually diminishing, and d'Alembert's feeling toward her was utterly devoid of sentiment. Among her women friends the maréchale de Luxembourg came nearer than any other to touch her heart, but Deffand herself said their bond of friendship was little more than an ancient habit. The others, she knew, were thoroughly insincere.

It was about the year 1760 that Deffand established a friendship which brought her into intimate relations with the most powerful man in France. The duc de Choiseul, whose intimacy with madame de Pompadour had raised him to the position of minister of foreign affairs, had gained an enviable reputation for sagacity in handling the country's relations with other powers and had amassed an enormous fortune as a reward for distributing public office among his friends. Though regarded by many as an adroit politician rather than a profound statesman, he enjoyed unbounded popularity because of his affability and his lavish entertainments. Deffand was always a little awed by his magnificence, and, in fact, it was the duchesse de Choiseul rather than the minister that aroused her deepest interest. Deffand was a distant relative of an earlier Choiseul, and in a moment of playfulness she pictured herself as the grandchild of the present duke. For the rest of her life this playfulness was continued and she always treated the youthful duchesse as a grandmother whose wisdom and instructions it was her natural duty to respect.

So far as externals went there was not much in common between the immature duchesse and her seventy-years-old grandchild. Choiseul's wife was an innocent little creature against whom scandal never raised its voice. Deffand once remarked that she would have loved her more if she had had some faults—she was too nearly perfect. Though she was always setting men's hearts on fire, her own escaped the flame. "The chief use of women," she observed, "is to curb men." In using the curb, however, she must have used a gentle hand, for everybody loved her and some thought it would have been wiser had she held her husband with a tighter rein. Deffand was drawn to her partly through a longing for repose. The youthful grandmother always was serene. Deffand, who was bored by her own existence, found untold comfort in the joyousness of her friend. In one thing, too, their natures were much alike—they allowed nothing to stand in the way of their emotions. The duchesse, it is true, would never admit the value of sentiment, and made a show of enjoying philosophical discussions—a little empty, as all such discussions are. Perhaps that was her method of curbing men. But her unwavering allegiance to her husband, and her lasting devotion to her poor old blind friend, show that philosophy was not the guiding principle of her life. Deffand, who hated to talk seriously, often went so far as to declare that she cared nothing for intellect. "Facts," she once said, "are surer than arguments, and sentiment is worth more than intelligence."

After ten years of almost daily intercourse the friendship of these two women was tested by a violent upheaval. Madame de Pompadour died and was succeeded in the king's affections by madame du Barry whom Choiseul had bitterly opposed. As a result the minister fell from power and was exiled to his château at Chanteloup on the Loire. To add to his distress no one was allowed to visit him without obtaining permission from the king, and few dared ask for such permission lest they incur the enmity of du Barry.

Deffand had special ground for apprehension, for she was drawing a pension which Choiseul had secured for her while madame de Pompadour was in power. It is much to Deffand's credit that she proposed to take the chance and was deterred only by the insistence of the duke. After a while the ban was removed, and Deffand did go out to Chanteloup. It was in May, 1772, that she made the trip. The bishop of Arras acted as her escort, and she was accompanied by her secretary, two lackeys, and her maids. She stayed five weeks. Everything was so grand it seemed to her like going to court, and she writes that she never had a moment's ennui till the visit was at an end. She found the "grandmother" more affectionate than ever and to all appearances in no way cast down by her lot. In spite of the loss of his emoluments the exiled minister was pouring out his money like water. In his magnificent palace he kept fifty servants, and twenty people were often seated at his table. There were eighty-five blooded cattle in his stables. He and his wife whiled away their time in riding, and in theatrical exhibitions in which he and his guests took part. They were both much touched by the sympathy of those who had known them in his days of power, and he erected on his grounds a stately pagoda on which were carved the names of all those who visited him in his exile. The duchesse declared that she had never been so happy in her life. The exile lasted four years till the death of Louis XV in 1774. Then the Choiseuls returned to Paris and the duke celebrated his return by giving an entertainment for all the servants of those who had stood by him in his disgrace. It was, of course, a joy to Deffand to have the Choiseuls in Paris, though she was never able to shake off her trepidation in the presence of the famous minister. Once, on his chiding her for always declining invitations to his suppers, she replied jocosely that she would accept if he would ask her three months in advance, as she needed time to prepare for his august presence.

One of the tragic episodes in the life of Deffand was her parting with Julie de Lespinasse. Coming to Paris almost as a waif, Julie's heart was filled with gratitude to the bene-

factress through whom she was given her first vision of
abundant life. The nightly gatherings at Saint-Joseph's
brought her into close relations with persons whose thoughts
were fixed on pleasurable ends. Although a bar sinister disfigured her escutcheon, she was conscious that the blood pul-
sating through her body was not a whit inferior to that of
her employer or of her employer's guests. That she would
make no effort to assert her right was written in the bond,
but her benefactress had not exacted a promise that Lespinasse would suppress the emotions that are inseparable
from youth. So far as we can learn she performed with
exactness the duties for which she was engaged. Deffand
wrote to a friend that she was every day more contented with
Lespinasse. Had she been able to use her eyes, she would
have seen things that would have given her less cause for
praise. Julie, though not exactly beautiful, was one of those
women to whom men instinctively are drawn, and it could
hardly be expected that the attention which they all showed
her would have left her completely cold. Deffand had warned
her that she had two intimate friends, Formont and d'Alembert, whom she loved passionately, not so much for their
charm or their friendship as for their absolute integrity.
There was also Turgot, later contrôleur général, of whom
Deffand wrote, "There was no one but he who really interested himself in me, who could advise me, who shared my
troubles. He was not tender or affectionate, but he was loyal
and solid." Between these men and Deffand there was a bond
of real friendship. They were talented men whom she rejoiced

to have about her not only because their companionship was cheering but also because they contributed to the prestige of her salon. Her relations with them were exceedingly cordial yet based entirely on intellectual confidence. When Julie came into the picture, a more exhilarating atmosphere permeated the apartment. Deffand still dominated the course of conversation, but before her sightless eyes there were often exhibitions of gallantry in which she had no part. No proof exists that Julie was yet guilty of any untoward behavior. She was under a heavy obligation to Deffand not only for lifting her out of obscurity but also for securing to her a modest pension from the king; and she had too much sense to run the risk of incurring her employer's wrath. But, as her subsequent history shows, she was a woman with a double heart, and as time wore on she grew less careful to conceal her duplicity. It is related, though not on unimpeachable testimony, that her admirers sometimes lingered with her in the antechambers while Deffand was kept fretting about their late arrival, and that this misbehavior finally came to Deffand's ears. Whether or not Deffand ever discovered any actual wrongdoing is uncertain, but, at any rate, after Lespinasse had been in her service about ten years, Deffand discovered that some of her dearest friends were paying marked attention to Lespinasse and it aroused her indignation to find that the young lady whom she had so abundantly befriended was beginning to outshine her in her own salon. The break seems to have reached its climax in a hasty quarrel in which both parties lost their tempers and used language which made it impossible for their cordial relationship to continue. Deffand's pride was touched and she told Julie to leave the house, at least for a while. After a few months Julie begged to be taken back, but Deffand replied that she could not do so till Julie had shown repentance for the cruel words which she had used to her. Meantime, d'Alembert's attentions to the young lady became so marked that Julie found she could get along without the protection of Deffand, and she opened a salon of her own which almost rivalled that of her benefactress.

To the end of her life Deffand did not relent. After the tragedy occurred she almost never mentioned Lespinasse. Twelve years later Julie died, and on the same day Deffand wrote a long letter to the duchesse de Choiseul; but in that letter she made no mention whatever of the death.

With the departure of Lespinasse, d'Alembert went completely out of Deffand's life, and it was largely on this account that Deffand sided against the encyclopédistes of whom d'Alembert was one of the leading spirits. The publication of the encyclopédie was one of the momentous events in French history. It paved the way for the Revolution. Starting merely as a scheme for making money, it became an effective moulder of public opinion. The director of the venture was a rather disreputable scholar named Diderot who had gained considerable fame through his philosophical writings as well as through the publication of a very indecent book, Les bijous indiscrets. Never would the encyclopédie have got the hold it did, had not Diderot secured as collaborators some of the most brilliant and original writers of the day. Voltaire, and Rousseau, and Montesquieu contributed a number of articles, as did also Turgot. D'Alembert wrote the preface, which declared that the purpose was to trace the origin of human knowledge and the relationship that existed among its various parts. The relation of art to science, of politics to religion, of morals to society, could not of course be discussed without resort to much fine-spun argument in which the contributors did not always agree, but they all began—and it is this that gave the book its importance—with the doctrine that the basis of all knowledge was the experience of the average man. There was no such thing as the supernatural. That of course was a direct blow to religion. The only guide to conduct was the prompting which the individual received from his own experience. So that each man's intellectual and bodily nature must tell him what he had a right to do. From that it is easy to see what a cogent argument one could offer for immorality. Anything which his nature dictated was right. There was no reason why a man's conduct should be subject to external restraint. Thus one was led to the conclusion that he should not be subject to governmental control.

As was to be expected the encyclopédie awoke the hostility of the authorities, and on two occasions the book was suppressed by the government on the ground that it set forth maxims tending to destroy the royal authority, to establish a spirit of independence and revolt, and, in obscure and equivocal language, to erect a substructure of error, of corrupt morals, and of irreligion and unbelief. Later the publication was allowed to continue, and it became a popular vehicle of thought among various classes of people. It pleased those who found moral restraint irksome and it appealed to those who were opposed to the rapacity of the clergy or to the inefficiency of the king.

It is proof of the soundness of Deffand's judgment that she scorned the encyclopédistes. Apparently she had no conception of the harmful effect which their doctrines were destined to have. But elaborate argumentation always irritated her. The proponents of these new ideas prided themselves on being called philosophers, and philosophy was to her utterly meaningless. To speak the truth, a great many of the articles in the encyclopédie, though not entirely meaningless, were utterly fanciful, and, after a few years of association with the movement, the wisest of the contributors became disgusted and dropped out. D'Alembert remained only long enough to establish his reputation as a leading scholar. Voltaire thought the dissertations were lacking in method. The article on woman he asserted must have been written by the lackeys of Gil Blas; and he wrote to Diderot, "I hope you will permit no more such articles as those on femme and fat, and no more such idle declamations, such puerilities and commonplaces." He said the encyclopédie was disfigured by a thousand ridiculous articles and schoolboy declamations.

To get a true picture of Deffand's views regarding the philosophers and indeed regarding many other matters one must study all her correspondence, for she never took pains to elaborate her ideas by long dissertations. She dealt much in epigrams and in sudden bursts of eloquence which came often from her pen with the force of an explosion. Many of her assertions seem to have been prompted by sentiment rather than by stern processes of reason. Especially was that true, as perhaps it always must be, in her judgment of people. She found delight in calling herself a cynic and the great chair in which she sat her tonneau, in imitation of Diogenes and his tub. In a moment of exasperation she ejaculated, "All men are fools or miscreants, most of them both," and she added that people were becoming greater fools every day. "At present," she said, "there is nothing but artifice, malice, extravagance." She declared that she spent her time "in tearing off the masks."

To be perfectly honest, there were plenty of masks that she was justified in tearing off. There has seldom been an age more artificial than that in which madame du Deffand lived. In politics, in literature, in conversation, you cannot seem to find anything really genuine. Louis XV himself was nothing but a sham. He pretended to govern the country but in reality he governed nothing: It was he who was governed, first by his mistresses, and then by the clergy and nobility. His financial accounting was utterly fictitious; the budget was never balanced, and there was no way of estimating what the expenditures of the government were likely to be. The persons who served under him vied with one another in the splendor of their establishments but many of them were bankrupt or would be as soon as they fell out of royal favor, and very few of them possessed any special qualifications for the offices which they had undertaken to fill. Society was made up largely of those who held these lucrative posts, supplemented by hangers-on who were dependent wholly on pensions which through someone's influence they were receiving from the king. These were the people who belonged to Deffand's set, and it is not strange that she should have sometimes revolted against their insincerity.

It must not be supposed, however, that she did not find much to commend. There are various degrees of perversity in the human race, and Deffand's skill in analyzing character enabled her often to discover sterling qualities in those whom a less discriminating observer might easily have regarded as altogether bad. Frequently, as in the case of Lespinasse, she allowed herself to become embittered by a personal affront. It may well be that she gave too much weight to her personal likes and dislikes. But she seldom failed to diagnose correctly the salient features of individual character. Among those whom she entertained at her apartment was the famous statesman Charles James Fox. Occasionally he would bring his friends around to Saint-Joseph's after supper was over and they would play cards for heavy stakes till dawn. Her infirmity of course debarred her from participation in this sport, but it did not prevent her from becoming familiar with the idiosyncrasies of her guests, and what she detected did not add to her esteem for Fox. She could find no point of contact with him. His only interests were politics and gambling, neither of which appealed to her. "He has not a bad heart," she says, "but he has no principles and no regard for those who have. He never troubles himself about the morrow. He is in dire poverty, with no possibility of paying his debts; but that makes no difference to him."

In 1773 she made the acquaintance of madame Necker, whose husband was reputed to be the richest man in France. The Neckers were protestants and not received in polite society, but she was often invited to supper at their house. At first she did not comprehend them. They lacked the polish to which she was accustomed. She was shocked by the noisy manner in which their household was conducted. Later, when she became accustomed to their brusqueness, she grew to appreciate their sterling qualities, and established almost an intimacy with madame Necker. "She is amiable, and not a fool or insipid—much better fitted for society than most of the ladies of the great world." Necker himself always failed to inspire her with confidence. She regarded him as a man of talent and absolutely honest, but when he was summoned by the king to straighten out the finances she doubted whether he would be successful. She said he was introducing all sorts of reforms which pleased the people, but that he was doing more harm than good.

It made her laugh to see her old friend Turgot, who had deserted her for Lespinasse, appointed contrôleur général. "Now you are all going to become encyclopédistes. Let us hope the people of the market-place will become so, too."

Turgot did not last long, however. He was dismissed and his post given to a friend of the duc de Choiseul. Deffand was overjoyed. She said Turgot was a man of good intentions but no sense, and moreover very ambitious and presumptuous.

As for du Barry, no color was black enough to paint her picture. She was a monkey, a parrot, with no mind of her own. "She rules everything, and is as insolent as she is stupid." And she quotes these verses about the queen and du Barry:

> "De deux Vénus on parle dans le monde:
> De toutes deux gouverner fut le lot;
> L'une naquit de l'écume de l'onde,
> L'autre naquit de l'écume du pot."

Louis XV she never liked. When he died, a verse was going the rounds which she was bold enough to quote:

> "Ci-git Louis le quinzième
> Du nom de bien-aimé le deuxième
> Dieu nous presérve du troisième."

The historian Edward Gibbon when in Paris was constantly at her house, and often took her out to supper. She found him entertaining but inclined to show off.

Regarding the maréchale de Luxembourg, who entered into her life more than any other woman, she sometimes expressed herself with unusual frankness. At one time she wrote, "I am only fairly comfortable with her. She wants to be important, sententious, epigrammatic—and she is merely tiresome." And to a friend who couldn't see what the two had in common she confided that their relations were simply a habit which had the appearance of a friendship. They certainly were a rather incongruous pair. Deffand's infirmity coupled with her straitened circumstances gave her a constant sense of dependence whereas the maréchale's wealth and exalted lineage rendered her free as air. She continued her life of gayety long after Deffand had been forced to give hers up. Deffand could never quite believe her friend was sincere though she was confident that the maréchale would never do anything unfair. Perhaps the clearest statement of Deffand's feelings is contained in the pen-portrait in which she said that Luxembourg "without being presumptuous dominates unconsciously everyone about her. She is faithful, discreet, and generous. People fear her rather than love her. She hates affectation." At any rate, whatever their feelings toward each other were, they clung to each other right up to the end, and when Deffand was eighty-three she wrote that Luxembourg was her best friend, and she added, "If in the past her faults have outweighed her good traits, they do not now. No one has a better heart, is more constant, or more charitable."

From a worldly point of view, at any rate, Luxembourg was the best friend Deffand ever had. Almost all of Deffand's intimates were connected in one way or another with the

maréchale's family. There was the marquise de Boufflers,
a relative of Luxembourg's first husband and one of the
clever women of her day. Apart from her inveterate taste for
gambling she was a delightful companion and her sparkling
wit enabled her to touch a chord that often vibrated in unison
with the sprightliness of Deffand. Deffand playfully called
her the "oiseau" because she was always on the wing. Ever
hovering about the marquise was the prince de Beauffremont,
whom Deffand found "sweet and easy to get along with. But
he has no principles, no sentiment. He never moves until
you pull the strings." Then there was the other marquise de
Boufflers, the gay and venturesome widow whom Deffand
called the "idol" because of the prince de Conti's infatuation
for her. When Conti died the marquise had no difficulty in
finding another lover to take his place. Deffand found her
entertaining, but could never quite forgive her for continuing her friendship with "the Lespinasse." Another of the
Luxembourg tribe was the maréchale de Mirepoix, also an
inveterate gambler. This lady seems to have been a sort of
fire-eater. The maréchale de Luxembourg couldn't endure
her, and Deffand who tried to keep on good terms with both
of them never dared to invite them to her supper parties
on the same day. Mirepoix also incurred the enmity of the
Choiseuls, and when the duc de Choiseul fell from power
she was given a place at court with a stipend of a hundred
thousand francs a year. While this lasted she was a little inclined to give Deffand the cold shoulder. But Deffand, much as
she regretted to see a feud spring up among her friends, never

lost her liking for the fiery maréchale and in one of her letters heaped upon her this rather extravagant praise: "Mirepoix is sweet and gentle, and the love that fills her heart shows itself in her face and gives to all her actions a peace and warmth which makes her loved by everybody." What kept her close to Deffand was that she was the sister of the prince de Beauvau, on whom the afflicted occupant of Saint-Joseph's leaned more dependently than on any other man she knew. Her "faithful prince," as the duchesse de Choiseul once called him, was a gentleman of quiet demeanor whose kindly assistance was always extended to persons in distress.

And surely he could have found no one better entitled than Deffand to his support. Her financial condition was always somewhat straitened. She had some income from the estate which she inherited from her mother and this was increased by a pension of six thousand francs per annum that Hénault secured her from the queen. This pension was cut down later to three thousand francs per annum. One of her friends generously offered to make up to her this loss, but she declined this offer and wrote that she still had an income of thirty-five thousand francs a year and that was enough for her to live on. This seems pretty modest in that extravagant age when the comtesse de la Marche was spending three hundred thousand francs to journey from Paris to her country place. Deffand's suppers must have often given her worry, but she certainly spent little on herself. Most people in society got up at ten, dined at two or three, and supped at nine. Deffand ordinarily spent the morning in bed, dispensed with dinner, and so had few expenses until the sun went down.

With her closed eyelids there was not much that she could do alone. Perhaps that was the reason why she had such a yearning for friendship. To her, friendship was the greatest boon in life. "Those who have no sentiment," she used to say, "avoid violent suffering, but they get no real pleasure." Other things fade away. "Friendship is the only passion that does not die with age." And the fact is she needed friends more than most of us. Many of the people about her she knew were not real friends, but with her a little friendship was better than none at all. "I shall persist to the end of my life in the mistake of believing that the only happiness in the world is to love and to be with the person one loves." She once wrote, "We all need love, or at least society." And she was not far from right, though it is pathetic to note how much she suffered in trying to satisfy her needs. There is a romance of friendship more touching sometimes than the romance of love. Often she almost gave up in despair. "Sometimes I think friendship is a chimera," and she constantly remarked that society was a dreadful bore. That came, of course, from her incapacity to take part in many of the things that amused others. Almost everybody was playing cards— and for tremendous stakes. A sarcastic English observer remarked there weren't fifty people in Paris who had any occupation other than gambling. Deffand went frequently to the opera and to the theater, but she made the comment—

and with perfect justice—that most of the plays performed in her time were insipid.

Almost the only other resources that Deffand had were writing letters and reading books. Soon after she became blind she secured the services of a man named Wiart as secretary. He was devoted to her heart and soul and remained with her twenty-seven years—in fact until her death. He was a most important personage in her household. The duchesse de Choiseul called him Deffand's governor. He read to her two or three hours a day and she dictated to him most of her letters, though she invented a frame which enabled her to write her most intimate letters with her own hand. In her library there were about two thousand books, and they were a great comfort to her. She said, "There are only two pleasures in the world for me—society and reading." With the aid of Wiart and her companion, mademoiselle Sanadon, she read almost everything that came out, but she was exceedingly critical of what she read. In a moment of exasperation she wrote, "I don't like authors, their taste, their knowledge, or their morals." She hated history and metaphysics. Nothing gave her real enjoyment except letters and romances. Of the latter she found nothing in French that compared with the English. She loved the portrayal of character in Tom Jones and Clarissa Harlowe. It seemed to her that the French romances were not true to life.

Some of her comments on human nature show real genius. Of a lady whom she knew slightly she remarked, "Her intellect is like space—it has no dimensions. She has no sentiment, no passion. She is like a flame that gives out no heat."

"Men do not love women for any merit they find in us but for the merit we find in them."

"Friendship cannot exist without confidence, and without confidence we are alone in the world."

"You English are subject to no rule or method. You let genius grow without forcing it to take this or that form. . . . We French are children of art."

"The English are strange beings. One can never understand them. Each one is original. There are no two alike. We are just the opposite. When you have seen one of our courtiers you have seen all."

"It is better to be a bad original than a good copy."

To a friend who had written in praise of youth she replied that in youth, charm and a lovely face take the place of intelligence; but that all attachments of youth are based on bodily impulses, and persons who form such attachments find old age nothing but a desert.

Of political matters she professed to be profoundly ignorant. When Russia and Prussia were coming to blows in 1772 she wrote, "These things are above my head." To be sure she took sides against the king of France in his quarrels with the parliaments, and she disliked his minister the duc d'Aiguillon, but that was only because he had displaced her friend Choiseul. "Public affairs," she said, "sometimes surprise me, but they don't interest me." At the end of 1772, when the brothers of the king were pardoned for their opposition and went back to court, she wrote, "Now we shall see

how the combat of the ferocious beasts will end. What a
delight it would be if they should all strangle one another."
In 1775, riots were breaking out all over France on account
of the scarcity of bread. Deffand comments on the fermentation that was going on everywhere, but she never suggests
a remedy. The American Revolution was at its inception, but
it drew from her only a passing comment. "I have heard no
one say that we are protecting America. I don't believe it,
but I am very ignorant, so that doesn't prove anything."
Franklin was then in Paris and she had him with his cap
and spectacles at her apartment. Among the persons that she
asked to meet him were a number of those who favored the
cause of the colonies. Her inclination led her to espouse the
English cause. "I am a royalist," she says, "though I don't
know why unless it is to please my friend the English ambassador. I don't understand these things." The fact is, she
belonged to that class of people who pave the way for revolution—who see that things are wrong but never cry out
against them. She was satisfied to let things drift. She hated
the artificial life of the society in which she was placed, but
didn't feel called upon to revolt against it. "I am not a
fanatic about liberty," was the way she put it. "I think it an
error to suppose liberty can exist in a democracy, as you
merely have a thousand tyrants instead of one. . . . We are like
sheep. We pasture tranquilly and you shear us a little close
while you are getting ready to cut our throats; but what
should we gain by rebellion?" That frame of mind was
characteristic of the times. All men's thoughts were busied

on just one thing—to get their share of the stream of money
that was flowing like water from the royal coffers.

There was one thing about Deffand for which she certainly
deserves no praise. She had the habit, like most people of her
time, of indulging in extravagant flattery of those in lofty
place, and of continuing on cordial terms with persons whom
she criticized behind their backs. Her letters to Voltaire are
weighted down with asseverations of admiration; yet in writing to the duchesse de Choiseul she says that Voltaire, at
any rate in the latter years of his life, was a greatly over-
rated man. But it must not be forgotten that her helpless condition made it imperative for her to keep open every avenue
of help. After Hénault's death she felt it more than ever
necessary to keep the friends she had. "I have always been
under the necessity of establishing myself and maintaining
my position. I have always had to lean on someone." She
admitted with perfect frankness that she had to tolerate many
persons for whom she had no respect.

In her continuous effort to keep afloat Deffand had to go
through many periods of deep depression, and occasionally
when dejected she would let some phrase escape which did
not express her genuine feelings. When she declared that
she could get no pleasure out of books she did not state things
exactly as they were. Who would not become weary if read
to for three or four hours every day? Though she talked
a good deal about ennui it may well be doubted whether she
differed much from those about her. Everybody was disgusted with the emptiness of society and wanted to escape

from it. Surfeited with pleasures, and having no serious business except the struggle to keep their place at court, most men—and women, too—spent their days in bed and their nights in gambling. The only thing that relieved the monotony of existence was going out to tiresome suppers and stuffing one's self with food. Even that had its drawback, for almost everyone was suffering from gout. Deffand prided herself above all else on being sincere, and she probably told the truth when she declared, "I detest the life that I am leading."

Still, she kept at it till the end. When she was seventy-six she gives the duchesse de Choiseul a record of her daily life. "I pass the night, dear grandmama, without sleep. As a rule I don't fall asleep till noon of the following day. Then I am read to for five hours. Sometimes I get up at five or six. Company arrives and I almost always have people here till nine—or till one in the morning if I sup at home. If I don't, I go out at nine."

Her vitality was nothing short of amazing. Here is a record of one week. Sunday she had fourteen persons at supper; Monday, stayed all day with Hénault and at midnight went out to supper; Wednesday, spent the evening with the English ambassador and stayed till midnight; Thursday, supped with Hénault, who had a number of guests; Friday, with Hénault, who was entertaining mesdames de Luxembourg, de Lauzun, and de Boufflers; Saturday, again with Hénault and a number of duchesses; and every evening called on her friend Crawfurt with whom she always found the Duke of Queensbury.

When seventy-two, we find her supping with the princesse de Beauvau, where she ran into the maréchale de Luxembourg and the marquise de Boufflers. She got home at four o'clock in the morning.

When eighty, she had at supper mesdames de Grammont, de Beauvau, de Luxembourg, de Lauzun, de Boufflers, and messieurs de Choiseul, de Beauvau, the ambassador from Naples, Saint-Priest, and Gibbon. The night before, she had supped with madame de La Vallière and then, at one in the morning, had gone round to the princesse de Beauvau's. A few days later she went to the opera where she enjoyed the music but found the recitative frightful.

When she was eighty-one, Beauvau supped with her while his wife was supping with the princesse de Poix. These two ladies, however, came around at half-past one and stayed till three.

After she reached the age of eighty-two she didn't go about much but still kept up her Wednesday and Friday suppers, often with as many as twenty guests, chiefly the old stand-bys—mesdames de Luxembourg, de Lauzun, de Boufflers, de Broglie, de Beauvau, de Cambis, de Mirepoix, together with four or five bishops and several members of the diplomatic corps. It was getting to be a good deal of an effort. "It is a torment to me to get up my supper parties. I go to a thousand troubles to bring together a fashionable gathering that bores me to death."

Say what you will, she must have had a charming personality to hold these people right up to the end. She could not have had the devotion of Pont-de-Veyle for fifty-five years and the affection of "grandmama" for twenty, had there not been something lovable about her. The famous Montesquieu wrote of her, "I love that woman with all my heart. She pleases me. She diverts me. There is not a moment's tedium when you are with her."

It is related of her that after she became blind her face retained all its delicate charm. She kept her eyelids completely closed and in talking she always turned her face to the person with whom she talked. Though everyone flattered her on account of the charm which pervaded her correspondence she was always modest about it. She said she knew her letters were superficial, and she added, "I don't know a word of grammar. My manner of expressing myself comes to me as a gift, and is wholly independent of rules." Yet she was not blind to the merits which she had. "When I compare myself with other women, I feel more respect for myself. I think I am more faithful and more sincere than any other. But I am weak."

When Deffand was sixty-eight years old one of the most gifted members of the literary coterie in London came over to Paris to buy rare porcelains. Among his intimates was George Augustus Selwyn, a brilliant but somewhat erratic Englishman who had spent much of his life in the French capital. Knowing that his friend enjoyed the society of entertaining women, Selwyn handed him a letter of introduction to the marquise du Deffand; and thus began a friendship

which absorbed Deffand's attention for the remaining fifteen years of her life.

Nature designed Horace Walpole to play a leading part in
world affairs. Of aristocratic birth, inheritor of ample means,
educated at Eton and Cambridge, with engaging manners
and almost unequalled skill in literary expression, he might
easily have taken rank with his distinguished father, the
great premier of England. But along with his ennobling
qualities there was a strain of less substantial impulses
which reduced him almost to the level of an eccentric dilettante. When he came into Deffand's life he was forty-nine
years of age and his habits had become fixed. He had settled
down as a bachelor in his artistic, though somewhat bizarre,
mansion called Strawberry Hill at Twickenham, near London, had sat in parliament for several sessions without
apparently taking any interest in public affairs, and had
done some rather desultory imaginative writing. His romantic nature had brought him into close intimacy with the poet
Gray and his love of irresponsibility had led him into companionship with the brilliant but reckless statesman Charles
James Fox. He had grown to look on life with the eyes of
a cynic.

At his very first meeting with Deffand he was completely
enthralled. Although she was twenty years his senior, her
vivacity aroused in him an exhilaration which he tried to
make himself believe he had suppressed for good and all.
"She is delicious," he wrote to a friend. "She retains all her
vivacity, wit, passions, and agreeableness, makes new songs

and epigrams and remembers every one of them that has been written in the last eighty years. She laughs at the clergy and philosophers. Her judgment is seldom wrong, but her conduct always wrong, for she is all love and hatred, still anxious to be loved—I don't mean by lovers."

He remained in Paris about six months, and was at her suppers twice almost every week. While there he told her that he loved her, but begged her never to mention his name to his friends. Immediately after he left she wrote him that no one could love him more tenderly than she did. "I will talk with you just as if we were tête-à-tête in front of the fire."

There was something in Walpole's make-up that rendered it impossible for him thoroughly to understand Deffand. In the portraits which we have of him there is a lack of virility in his face. His eyes were beautiful, but almost effeminate, and convey the impression that he could not comprehend exactly the varied character of love. His knowledge of the French tongue was meager and his acquaintance with French women limited, thus leading him to give a wrong interpretation to Deffand's words. Stupidly enough, he imagined there was something sensuous in her feelings, and it irritated him, coming from a woman of sixty-eight. So she had to explain: "Anything that resembles love is hateful to me, but I am made for friendship. My heart was never made for anything but that." Not satisfied, he wrote her that she was indiscreet and romantic. "Yes," she replied, "I am indiscreet, but surely you cannot imagine that you have turned my head. . . . You may be Abélard, if you wish, but I could never be Héloïse." He was very fond of the letters of the marquise de Sévigné, and she tried to make him understand her feelings by referring to those letters. "Read them again and again," she exhorts, "and see if friendship cannot make one feel and say things a thousand times more tender than all the romances in the world."

The following year Walpole wrote her that he was coming again to Paris and solely to see her. She wrote back that she would always be in her little cell ready to receive him, but that he would be free to do anything he pleased. "What a sad thing for me that I have formed such a feeling of friendship for you, and how little you have understood me when you have interpreted it as love. I do not love you just because I esteem you, nor because I seem to have found in you the qualities for which I have searched in vain these fifty years. That is what has charmed me and made it impossible for me not to attach myself to you."

He arrived on August 23rd, 1767, and rushed right to Saint-Joseph's to have supper with her. On October 9, 1767, he left Paris, and she wrote him the same day, "What of it if one is old and blind?—If a woman's heart is full to the brim, she lacks nothing but the object on which her heart is set, and if that object responds to her feelings there is nothing more to be desired."

Deffand had now reached a state of ecstasy which wholly changed her character. She had found her hero, her god, before whom she was eager to obliterate herself. She called

him her tutor to whom she looked for instruction in the
conduct of her life. Her letters to him followed each other
in quick succession and were filled with such expressions of
adoration that he became alarmed; and he kept enjoining
upon her to restrain the extravagance of her expressions.
She begged him to pardon her, for she was only a woman.
"Je suis femme, très-femme, femmelette." He wrote back,
"If you want our friendship to last, give it a less tragic tone."
Following his instructions, she resorted to pleasantry, and
wrote him that he must write to her regularly every two
weeks. "If you don't I shall say to my secretary: 'Pack up
and fly to London. Proclaim in all the streets that you come
from me, that you have orders to go and live with Horace
Walpole, that he is my tutor, that I am his pupil, that I am
passionately in love with him, that I am going to establish
myself at Strawberry Hill, and that there is no scandal which
I shall refrain from stirring up."

This jollity pleased him no better. He wrote her that her
letters were ridiculous and she replied she knew they were.
"Has an old sybille, shut up in her cage and seated on her
tonneau, a right to talk familiarly to Apollo, a philosopher,
in short the only man of the era?" To allay his anxiety she
wrote that she was old enough to be his mother, and added,
"I regret deeply that I am not." Lest he think he was coming
to be under an obligation to her she wrote him, "Whatever
I receive from you will come as a favor and not as the pay-
ment of a debt. . . . I want nothing from you except to keep
you as my best friend till my last breath." She understood

him better probably than he understood himself. His character was full of contradictions, and she wrote and told him so. "You are sincere and good, you are variable but constant, you are hard but sensitive, yes, very sensitive, whatever you may say."

In 1768 he wrote her an irritating letter denouncing her constant talk of friendship. She replied, "In God's name, my tutor, stop your declamations about friendship. Let us not torment each other, I by vaunting what you detest, and you by blaming what I esteem. Let us banish friendship. But let us not forget its place of exile, lest we have need of it later."

This harsh decree was never carried to fulfillment. Though Deffand strove to modify her language, friendship breathed through every word she wrote. Once she reminded him that they had taken an oath never to indulge in friendship. "Heaven is witness that I do not love you, but nothing can prevent me from finding you most amiable." In spite of constant denials both of them realized the depth of their attachment. Scarcely a week passed by without their each communicating with the other. Meantime Walpole was working on a publication from the Strawberry Hill Press of a tragedy composed by Deffand's protector Hénault.

On August 15th, 1769, he came again to Paris, and gave this record of his reception: "My dear old woman is in better health than when I left her. . . . She and I went to the boulevards last night after supper and drove about there till two in the morning. We are going to sup in the country this evening and are to go to-morrow night at eleven to the puppet-show." She had secured his lodgings for him, and he writes that she was his best and sincerest friend. "She never leaves anything undone which can give me satisfaction." For the time being there was no rancor on his part and nothing but gentleness on hers. She tells a friend that Walpole is now satisfied with her and finds her less romantic. It was he that was now letting his pen run wild. In a letter to the duchesse de Choiseul he calls her "grandmama," excusing himself on the ground that he was Deffand's husband.

No sooner was she out of his sight than he began to bark again. He wrote her that she was vain, tyrannical, and indiscreet, that she would not believe a man had any heart unless he followed her into her bedroom. She answered that she had been indiscreet, but was now chastened; that she was certainly neither vain nor tyrannical. The poor woman hardly dared to say anything for fear of offending him. "I don't dare to make reflections; I don't know whither they would lead me, and it is so easy to displease you." Sometimes after writing him a long letter she would throw it into the fire because she saw something in it that he might not like. Occasionally she let it go though it contained words which he had forbidden. "I regard your friendship as the greatest good-fortune of my life. I would sacrifice everything else in the world to keep it."

In 1771 he came to Paris again, but stayed only a couple of weeks. Deffand took him about a great deal, but her late parties tired him out. After he left she was terribly dejected and wrote him, "I am conscious of the approach of old age. Loss of memory, inability for long application. . . . Everyone I see here dries up my soul. I find no virtue, no sincerity, no simplicity, in anyone. I find myself tied by fate to people who detest one another."

In 1772 his fault-finding was so incessant that she had to beg him to be more gentle with her. "When I receive a letter from you filled with reproaches, suspicion, coldness, I am unhappy for a week." She wrote him that she had learned to be docile, "but I am like a child; I need to be caressed and given a bon-bon." It was all of no avail. When she returned from Chanteloup, she received a succession of bitter letters from him, which made her suspect that he wished to bring their intimacy to a close. In one of those letters he had said, "I don't want any slaves . . . I don't love anyone but myself, and you don't love anyone but yourself; so we can never agree." She returned the letter to him. "Very well," she said, "we don't agree. So let us terminate a correspondence which has been nothing but a persecution to you." He appears to have accepted her decision. A couple of months later she regretted the breach and wrote him, "Let us make peace. Let us forget the past." This letter brought about a renewal of their correspondence, but from that date she gave up all hope of ever softening his heart.

In truth, there was no hope. On March 30, 1773, he wrote, "I have no more to say, madam. I see the impossibility of two natures so opposed as yours and mine coming to an agreement. I shall make no further effort to render agreeable a relationship with which by tormenting me you have made me disgusted. Let it take its own course. . . . If you do me the honor to write me letters requiring an answer, I will answer them. Otherwise you may dispense with my writing, for I do not see the necessity of a regular correspondence when both of us are so little satisfied with it."

On April 13th, 1773, he wrote, "After being thoroughly disgusted, one does not easily get back his good humor. I admit that I am always expecting new persecutions, and that robs our correspondence of all pleasure. . . . I regard this end of our liaison as unavoidable and I become each day more ready to give it up."

In November, 1773, he wrote, "With all possible intelligence and charm, you are unwilling to be contented with anything. You want to go chasing after a being that doesn't exist, and which your knowledge of the world ought to tell you doesn't exist, that is to say, a person who is solely and absolutely attached to you and who enjoys only one subject of conversation."

In April, 1774, she had written him she was thinking of going into a convent to shake off her loneliness. He wrote back that as she couldn't read she would find no satisfaction in that life . . . what she needed was company, not solitude.

In February, 1775, he became so ashamed of his treatment of her that he asked his friend General Conway to try to persuade her to let him have his letters back. She assented without a murmur. "You will have enough," she says, "to light your fires for a long time if you add to yours all those you have received from me. That would be only fair, but I leave it to your prudence. I shall not follow the example of distrust which you have shown me." He did not have the courtesy to take this hint. Of all his letters—about eight hundred of them—only nineteen escaped the flames. All of hers were preserved, and published after his death.

Her idol was now shattered, and she felt at liberty to tell him frankly what he had meant to her. This was what she wrote: "It is true that I find you a very singular man. You have good reason to say that our characters differ. Yours is incomprehensible to me. I cannot understand what pleasure you can get from solitude, or what charm you find in all your inanimate objects, or how you can prefer the grand world to intimate society. I grant that society hardly satisfies, but one always hopes that it will. I believe I have already told you that to me friendship is the main thing. One cannot always find gold, but he can find nuggets that give hope. You are proof of that. I have not found in you what I desire, but I have found in you something better than what I have found elsewhere. Your indifference comes nearer to friendship than all the assertions of friendship which I find about me."

And again: "You are right in saying that age and experience have taught me nothing. Age has disfigured me; and experience has disgusted me with the world—though it has not deprived me of the need of society. It is more necessary to me than ever. You cannot prevent me from regretting the loss of my poor friend Pont-de-Veyle. He listened to me and responded. He loved me more than he loved anyone else. He needed me and if all the world had abandoned me he would have remained faithful. He had a knowledge of the world which, though not profound, was sufficient. Too much penetration is sometimes an evil. There is danger in going too deep. We must sometimes skim along the surface."

One cannot read this calm analysis of the difference between her feelings and those of Walpole without realizing that Deffand was endeavoring to temper justice with mercy. She knew that Walpole had traits which were utterly ignoble and prevented him even from approaching her ideals. In one of her celebrated pen-portraits she had said of him, "The fear of being feeble makes him hard. He is always on his guard against his feelings. He will sacrifice his own interests for his friends, but he refuses them little attentions. If he has a weakness, it is his fear of ridicule, which makes him sub-servient to the opinion of fools." Even that estimate was all too charitable. He had been in the early years of their acquaintance almost her lover, calling her often "ma petite femme." He knew that in spite of her caustic criticisms she had an exceedingly gentle heart. He had a few modest friends and dependents in Paris whom he asked Deffand to aid, and their letters to him are filled with expressions of gratitude for her help. He was under great obligations to her for enter-taining him and introducing him to her friends. When he published his edition of the mémoires of the comte de Gram-mont he asked her to write the preface and sign it with her name. She wrote the preface but refused to allow him to use her name, because it might make him appear ridiculous to his friends. "You know me well enough to know that I want no praise." But he dedicated the work to her in these words: "To madam . . . The editor dedicates this edition to you as a monument of his friendship, admiration, and respect for one whose graces, intelligence, and taste remind the present age of the age of Louis XIV." He knew that she was poor, and blind, and delicate, and that she was exceedingly affectionate and emotional. He knew that her whole heart was wrapped up in him. Yet, when the glamour of their earlier intimacy had worn off, he treated her not only with coldness but with scorn. When a man's or a woman's sentiments have so changed that it is no longer possible without deceit to exhibit the ardor of an all-possessing love, it may be that it is honorable to call a halt, but in Walpole's case it was not so. He kept going to Paris to enjoy the hospitality of his dear old friend, as he constantly calls her, but in the intervals he heaped nothing but abuse upon her. Here was a man who boasted of his gentility, who surrounded himself at Strawberry Hill with the most artistic things that money could buy, who deemed himself a pattern of delicacy and refinement, and yet who permitted himself for fifteen years to beat down a sensitive and afflicted woman, and in writing to her to use language framed purposely to chill her affections and to wound a heart which he knew was filled with nothing but the tenderest feelings for him. He may have been irritable, he may have dreaded ridicule, but that is never reckoned an excuse for being brutal.

Deffand had now reached the age of seventy-eight, and there was nothing more for which she cared to live. Still, she could not voluntarily close a correspondence which had meant to her so much. Both she and Walpole believed her life was near its end and in the summer of 1775 he came once more to Paris to pay her a final visit. His record of that visit shows that though her heart was broken she was determined not to weary him with her grief. She kept him busy every minute with suppers and trips into the country. Her suppers lasted till two or three in the morning, and at one of the suppers which she gave for him she had the duc de Choiseul, the duchesse de Grammont, the prince and princesse de Beauvau, the princesse de Poix, the maréchale de Luxembourg, the duchesse de Lauzun, the duc de Gontaut, the duc de Chabot, and the Italian ambassador Caracciole. In characterizing her at this period, Walpole wrote, "One needs the activity of a squirrel and the strength of Hercules to keep up with her."

For five years more her marvellous vitality kept her going, and down almost to the end scarcely a week elapsed in which she and Walpole did not communicate with each other. But the tenor of her letters was now completely changed. She writes almost nothing about herself except in connection with personages about whom he had told her he would like to be informed. She lets him understand that her letters are to be little more than a gazette.

On the twenty-second of August, 1780, she wrote him that she had become so feeble that she could no longer stand. "I think my end is approaching. I haven't strength enough to be afraid, and, as there is no chance of my ever seeing you again, I do not care to live. . . . Amuse yourself, my friend, as well as you can. Don't trouble yourself about me. We have long been lost to each other. We could never have expected to see each other again. You will miss me, for it is always a pleasure to know that one is loved."

On the twenty-third of September she was dead.

MADAME de STAËL

✳

I⊤ ɪs impossible to review the career of Napoleon Bonaparte and not be impressed by the extraordinary influence that he had in developing the character of the French people. The nation is still governed by the code of law which he promulgated. The military spirit which in his day permeated all classes of the people has never been swept away. The confidence which the people have in themselves as a nation is as strong as when Napoleon was at the height of his power. Every Frenchman has inherited his indomitable will. An illustration of Napoleon's determination to have his way at all costs is furnished by his treatment of madame de Staël. So long as he was on the throne he never permitted her to come to Paris. To a woman of her social prominence that prohibition caused a bitter pang, and had much to do with shaping her career.

SHE is a sovereign from whose dominion the great men that surround her have no escape, for she chains them to her by a sort of magic." So spoke one of the scholars who frequented madame de Staël's princely château at Coppet, and his testimony as to her power of fascination is corroborated by many of those with whom she came in touch. Among her admirers were some of the most distinguished statesmen of her day, and all agree there was a charm about her personality which no one could resist. Though she laid no claim to beauty, the warmth of her emotions and the vivacity of her conversation kept everyone enthralled. Words flowed

from her lips in a perfect torrent, and at the height of her
fame she was known as the most brilliant talker in all
Europe.

There are those who think of madame de Staël only as
the friend of Benjamin Constant. That was but one phase in
the varied life of this extraordinary woman. She was an
active participant in the bloody scenes of the French Revolution; she did more than anyone else to relieve the sufferings
of the refugees; and she was a celebrated—some say the most
celebrated—imaginative writer of her time.

Fortune smiled upon her in her early years. She was the
only child of Jacques Necker, reputed to be the richest man
in France. When she was six years old her father retired from
business and loaned two million francs to the French government merely as an act of generosity to the country in
which his fortune had been made. Four years later, the national finances having gone from bad to worse, he was asked
by Louis XVI to formulate a plan of economic relief. As
Necker was a native of Switzerland, and moreover a protestant, which made it impossible for him to become a citizen
of France, many regarded him as an unfit person to be entrusted with the government's affairs; but his reputation as an
able financier outweighed all other considerations and about
a year after his services were first enlisted he was given the
important office of contrôleur général.

Shortly before this period Voltaire and Rousseau had been
flooding society with doctrines about the people's rights.
England had already become permeated with the new ideas

and the salons of Paris were beginning to take them up. Necker, as a protestant, was not an ardent advocate of vested rights and no sooner had he entered upon his public duties than he urged the king to summon the états généraux in order that they might adopt measures to lessen the burden of taxation. By this proposal he incurred the wrath of those in power and after five years of service was forced to resign. Seven years later, however, when the king decided to summon the états généraux, he was recalled.

Meantime his daughter, Anne-Louise-Germaine Necker, had grown into womanhood. Her father, though relegated to private life, was still regarded by many as the only person who could save the country from disaster, and his palatial home in Paris was frequented more and more by those who were out of touch with the reckless extravagance of the court. At Coppet on the borders of Lake Geneva her father owned a stately residence where he was in the habit of spending his summers and there she grew up, mingling with her father's distinguished guests and amazing them by her extraordinary vivacity and the charm and brilliancy of her conversation. Young as she was, there was always a ready audience when she was moved to speak, and few could hear her without being electrified by the force and originality of her ideas.

Necker himself regarded her as a prodigy and made no effort to restrain the manifestation of her talent. So she grew into maturity with the conviction that she was destined to play a leading part in the intellectual and social doings of her time.

Along with her mental development came a violent awak-
ening of the heart. She was by nature a child of exuberant
emotions. Her adoration of her father knew no bounds and
as she ripened into womanhood the vehemence of her feelings
tinctured all her thoughts. At twelve she had written a number of stories of which the basic theme was love. She went
into ecstasies over the English novelists of whom her favorite
was Richardson. Later, in looking back upon her childhood,
she declared, "The elopement of Clarissa was the main incident of my youth."

As the greatest heiress in Europe there were many suitors
for her hand. One of them was Louis de Narbonne of whom
she at one time wrote, "He was the first and only man I have
ever loved." Another was William Pitt whom she met while
he was on a vacation at Fontainebleau. She discouraged his
attentions because, as she declared, she could never give up
France.

The final choice fell upon a man who was selected by her
father for reasons that were wholly prudential. Necker's high
repute as a financier, along with his universally acknowledged integrity, had led to his being appointed to the most
important administrative position in France, but his religious
scruples had kept him from being duly recognized at court
and this had always rankled in his breast. When Germaine
was only fourteen she had met baron de Staël-Holstein, then
Swedish chargé d'affaires in Paris, and he had sought her
hand. It did not look like a particularly brilliant alliance,
and Necker was not inclined at first to give his assent. After

a while, however, it occurred to him that if de Staël, who was a protestant, could secure the appointment of Swedish ambassador, Germaine by becoming his wife could retain her religion and yet be entitled to participate in all the functions of the court. As the baron was heavily in debt and wholly unable without assistance to maintain the position of ambassador, the plan necessitated a liberal provision by Necker. Arrangements were finally agreed upon, and de Staël secured the post. Strangely enough, we have no record to show how far Germaine was active in furthering this plan. It may be that she was dazzled by the prospect of gaining an influential position in the social world of Paris, or it may be that she assented in order to comply with the wishes of a father whom she adored. At any rate the marriage was solemnized in 1786, and the couple took up their residence at the Swedish embassy in the rue de Bac three years before Necker was recalled to the ministry of finance.

There is abundant proof that Germaine entered into this marriage without any love in her heart. On the very day of taking her vows she wrote to her mother a letter filled with foreboding and without even mentioning the man to whom she was giving herself. Some of her friends foresaw that there could be nothing but discord between them. Madame de Boufflers wrote to the king of Sweden, "I wish I could think that de Staël will be happy, but I cannot believe it." She felt that Germaine lacked tact and knowledge of the world, and was too confident of her own judgment. In this madame de Boufflers was correct. Germaine was always assertive and at

this stage of her career the adulation that came to her because of her undeniable talent had so raised her self-esteem
that she could not have been a suitable wife for anyone. And
the breach was widened when she found that she was linked
to a man greatly her inferior in intellectual gifts.

In one respect, however, the marriage gave her intense
satisfaction. As wife of the Swedish ambassador she became
an important personage and was afforded opportunity to express herself with authority on public affairs. She was always
more or less theatrical, and it tickled her vanity to pose as a
leader in the diplomatic set. The statesmen summoned to her
salon stood aghast at the flood of eloquence that poured from
the lips of their youthful hostess, though it may well be
doubted whether she did not take too seriously their apparent
sympathy with her ideas. Her insatiable eagerness to play a
rôle brought her sometimes into a position where she placed
too high a value on the importance of her effort. Not satisfied
with the modest contribution of her husband, she deluged the
Swedish king with letters devoted mainly to rehearsing the
incidents of her own progress in the social world. Of a dinner
to which she was invited by Marie Antoinette she wrote, "The
king and queen both received me graciously; the queen told
me she had long wished to make my acquaintance. The dinner
was more splendid than had ever before been given for an
ambassadress." It was certainly a demoralizing life. As she
admits, utter recklessness pervaded everything. All the men
about her, including her husband, were ruining themselves by
gambling. Political offices were largely owned by the nobility

and it was reported that four thousand of them were being bought and sold. The unsavory episode of the diamond necklace, in which the queen and cardinal de Rohan were implicated, had poisoned men's minds regarding those of high estate. Cagliostro and Mesmer, both of them arch-impostors, were deluding prominent members of society and creating a widespread belief in occult manifestations.

After the recall of Necker his daughter transferred her salon to the house of her distinguished father, and this salon soon became a forum for the spread of liberal ideas. Rousseau's doctrines were on everybody's lips and Germaine came to be known as the most vigorous champion of the people's rights. She may not have realized whither her admiration for Rousseau was leading her. It was not till some years later that Napoleon declared, "Without Rousseau there would have been no revolution."

It could hardly be expected that Germaine's enthusiasm for Rousseau's political notions would not in time lead her more or less into agreement with his views on other things. In proclaiming the rights of individuals Rousseau laid stress upon the propriety of taking nature as our guide and of giving free rein to our impulses. In some of his imaginative writings he made light of lapses from the path of strict morality, excusing them on the ground that they were expressions of one's individuality. In 1788, when Germaine was only twenty, she published her first important book, and from passages in that book it is easy to detect that she was coming to look with complacency upon the relaxation of personal restraint. She had not yet reached the view that passion justifies everything, but she was getting perilously near it.

When Necker was recalled to power in 1788 he was given all the prerogatives of premier and became the idol of the people. The treasury was virtually empty and owing to a long succession of scanty crops many were perishing of hunger. Necker refused all salary and furnished a large sum from his own pocket to provide the people with food. To all intents and purposes he was the governing power and Germaine drank the cup of glory to the full. She was now convinced that it lay with her to usher in the great epoch of liberty which seemed to her at hand. One of her contemporaries wrote, "Among the remarkable and attractive members of the younger generation the baronne de Staël in particular exhibited such pungency and eloquence that very few could enter the lists against her. She not only surprised, she convinced and carried away, her hearers." As events proved, she wholly misconceived the direction in which things were to travel. She looked for a millennium based on the old régime but in which the people would be voluntarily granted the rights to which they were entitled by the laws of nature. It was a fantastic picture. Still, the baronne was only twenty-two.

In the next three years this brilliant, ambitious, headstrong young woman learned much about the ways of men. She learned that liberty of individual action could not be held within the narrow barriers which she had framed; that new rights cannot be granted without stimulating a desire for revenge because so long withheld; and that moderate counsel gets scant hearing when passions have been aroused. Her eyes were partially opened when her adored father, two months after the états généraux began their sessions, was forced to hand his resignation to the king.

Necker withdrew to Brussels where he was joined soon after by the baron and baronne de Staël. Then in a few days came the fall of the Bastille, followed on the next day by the emigration of the nobility including all of Germaine's dearest friends. The populace demanded the recall of Necker and he returned to Paris with Germaine. But it was too late. The assemblée nationale had taken control of everything, and the king's sole function was to sign such documents as the legislative body laid before him. Germaine could now see clearly enough to what her enthusiasm for democracy had led. The person on whom she chiefly pinned her faith was Talleyrand, now a member of the assemblée nationale. His serenity never left him even when surrounded by the angry mob. But his political sagacity stood in the way of his giving her much help. So long as the future was uncertain she could not prevail upon him to take a definite stand.

Necker hung on for another year, doing his best to pacify the people, but in 1790 the radical element so increased in power that he saw there was no longer hope of keeping the monarchy alive. So he retired from public life and never returned to it again. His daughter's devotion to him continued after he was gone. In her salon she went on striving to salvage the remnants of the old régime. With all her love of liberty she hated to part with the ceremonial and glitter of her palmy days. Gouverneur Morris, who visited her salon, wrote, "Her home is a kind of Temple of Apollo, where the men of wit and fashion gather twice a week for supper and once a week—sometimes oftener—for dinner." He found her clever, but she seemed to him conceited, and a coquette.

Even the fall of Necker could not check the astonishing vitality of Germaine. Though scarce a day went by without some new attack on those she cherished, she never faltered in rushing to their defense. When others dared not receive them they always found asylum in her house. Say what you will about her vanity, no one has ever ventured the assertion that she was not brave. With voice and pen she denounced the brutality of those in power, and every effort to silence her only added to the vehemence of her tongue. By one of her contemporaries she was characterized as the Bacchante of the Revolution.

Gossips were already busy with innuendoes about her private life, and people were talking much of her intimacy with Talleyrand, Ségur, and especially Narbonne. At one time there were rumors that she visited Narbonne's camp, clad in male attire. Narbonne was young, handsome, and immoral. He was believed by many to have been a natural son of Louis XV. He was a widower and though an officer in the army was an ardent supporter of the Revolution. He and Talleyrand, as well as Ségur and La Fayette, were constantly at the Swedish embassy, hovering about Germaine. All were talking democracy, though royalists at heart.

In 1791 de Staël went back to Sweden, unaccompanied by his wife. Later he returned to Paris, but she appears to have been indifferent both to his coming and to his going. The truth is, he had never been an important factor in her life. Who could, in fact, have had much influence upon a self-sufficient young woman like Germaine? De Staël was not altogether a nonentity, but he was no match for his restless and overpowering wife. In a scandalous pamphlet published in Paris he was pictured as the deceived husband while Talleyrand and Narbonne played the leading parts. Possibly the picture was overdrawn, but Germaine had only herself to blame if such rumors did her wrong. Both Talleyrand and Narbonne were noted for their gallantries, and her undeniable intimacy with them could not but arouse suspicion.

All the old families were now fleeing from France and the Swedish embassy was doing all it could to help them to escape. Germaine's bustling activity never had better opportunity to show its worth. Four thousand refugees were clustered along the Rhine, ready to join the foreign armies when they began their attack on France. Narbonne was now minister of war and the queen wrote, "So Narbonne is minister at last. What joy and glory for madame de Staël, who can now dispose of armies!" Germaine sided with the man she loved in spite of the wishes of her friends who would have been glad to see the enemy enter Paris. Whatever her expectations were, they failed of realization, for Narbonne was soon deprived of his command. Roland was now at the helm, and Germaine's influence was at an end. His wife had never liked Germaine whom she thought frivolous ever since she had detected her sending missives from the diplomatic gallery to deputies whom she knew. A coquette Germaine surely was, but when her country's interests were at stake she bravely advocated what she thought was right. She stood for the monarchy so long as it lasted. After it had fallen, she did not believe it ought to be restored.

Meantime Necker was imploring her to seek refuge at Coppet, which she was loath to do. She was thrilled by the excitement of her life in Paris and hated what she termed "the infernal quietude" of Coppet.

In July, 1792, the people were getting ready to break into the Tuileries and put the king and queen to death. At the risk of her own life Germaine devised a scheme to save them from the fury of the mob. She planned to buy an estate in Dieppe and have the royal couple carried to that city in disguise. They were then to be transported secretly to England. The project failed because the king and queen refused to flee.

Germaine was in Paris on August 10th, 1792, when the storm broke. The Tuileries were invaded and the king and queen were seized. Many of Germaine's friends were slaughtered on that awful day. She tried to cross the Seine from her home in the rue de Bac and rescue any that had not been killed, but she found the bridges barred. After dark she succeeded in getting across, but all her friends who had been able to escape were already hiding in different corners of the town.

No one dared to make a prediction as to the future or guess where the next blow would fall. As the wife of an ambassador Germaine had hitherto felt secure, but the fall of the monarchy took away the protection afforded to ambassadors, and their former relations with the king made them a special object of hatred to the infuriated people. Most of the embassies, in fact, were closed and those that still functioned were under suspicion because it was believed they were harboring citizens who wanted to escape from France. Germaine's husband was no longer an ambassador, but she had incurred the wrath of the revolutionary government by her outspoken advocacy of the old régime, and her house was searched to see if she were sheltering any individuals whom the authorities wished to hold. As a matter of fact, Montmorency and Narbonne were with her when the officers arrived, and Narbonne was one of those whom the government wanted because of his former intimacy with the king. How she managed to appease the officers has never been divulged, but in some way Narbonne escaped arrest and a few days later she secured for him a passport which enabled him finally to make his way to England.

Her lover saved, there was no further reason why Germaine should stay in Paris, and on September 2nd, just as the massacres began, she started for Switzerland, taking with her the abbé Montesquieu disguised as her servant. Her coach was stopped and she was taken before Robespierre, where she insisted upon her right, as the wife of a former ambassador, to depart. After several hours' delay she was allowed to go, and a few days later she arrived at Coppet.

She found her mother dying and the house encumbered with refugees. The place was so depressing that she stayed only long enough to give birth to her second child; and in December, 1792, she went to Surrey, England, where Narbonne and some of her other friends were gathered. Her four months' stay in Surrey brought her into contact with many intellectual people, among them Frances Burney, the author of Evelina. Germaine was the nucleus of this little coterie, though her unconventional manner of living kept some of the choicest spirits away. One of the women, herself a clever writer, remarked that if she were a queen she would command madame de Staël to talk to her all day long. Another commented on her unceasing activity, her open-heartedness, and her loyalty to her friends.

The winter over, she returned to Switzerland. Her husband, who had been again in Paris, joined her at Coppet and remained there with her till the end of the year. Many of the friends who had sojourned with her in England followed her to Switzerland and visited her from time to time. Much as she hated the repose of Coppet, it was much better that she should be there than amidst the carnage that was going on in Paris. It was the year of terror in which the guillotine had its daily victims and the king and queen were carried to the scaffold. Germaine had tried to avert this brutal act by publishing a defense of the queen—a magnanimous effort on the part of one to whom the queen had furnished many evidences of ill will.

More successful was her work in saving her old friend Montmorency. With the aid of false passports and by expending a large amount of money she enabled him to escape. At the same time she was busy at Coppet providing a resting-place for great numbers of refugees who were scurrying out of France. A distinguished man who met her about this time at Lausanne remarked that she would have been adorable had she not tried to be extraordinary. He thought her clever except when she tried to appear so. "Her head," he asserted, "has been ruined by philosophical doctrines, but her heart is unspoiled."

In this year Gibbon, who had spent most of his life at Lausanne, and had been a lifelong admirer of her mother, went back to England, where he died in January, 1794. This was a bitter blow to Germaine, as was also the death of her mother which occurred a few months later.

In 1794, with the fall of Robespierre, the reign of terror ended, and then began a new phase in the tempestuous life of Germaine. Narbonne had grown tired of her exuberance and had passed out of her life. There was no breach between them and their intimacy had probably grown as irksome to her as to him. Love of excitement and the imminence of danger had come to be all that kept them together; and now that peace was restored both realized that they had no longer much in common. Still, the passing of Narbonne left a void in her existence, and it was while she was in a state of moral lassitude that she found the man who really, more than any other, touched the deep recesses of her heart.

Benjamin Constant was twenty-seven and she was twenty-eight when they first met, on September 19th, 1794. He was a handsome, brilliant, and dissipated young man, without occupation, and was living on his father's estate in the neighborhood of Lausanne. He had called upon her at Coppet, mainly out of curiosity to see whether his famous neighbor was as interesting and original as everybody said. She was not in when he called, but later in the day he encountered her carriage on the road and she offered to drive him back to Lausanne. There they supped together, breakfasted, dined, and supped together the next day, and were together again on the following morning. He was completely fascinated and a few days later wrote that he had seldom met a woman with so charming a combination of characteristics, brilliant, sympathetic, kindly, affable. "To me she is the whole world . . . One who has met her can expect no greater happiness anywhere." Such language seems a little extravagant, though perhaps not altogether surprising from the pen of one who was sometimes spoken of as "Benjamin the Inconstant."

Her feelings toward him were far more complicated. She was a creature of impulse, accustomed to do whatever came into her head without much thought of consequences, and it is more than likely that her intimacy with Constant owed its beginning to a revolt against the tedium of her life among the refugees at Coppet. But her liaison with Constant was much too lasting and too fruitful in the development of both their intellects to justify the assertion that it was chiefly based on passion. One of the most propelling forces in Germaine's make-up was insatiate ambition. For eight years she had striven to play a leading part in the political events of France and had not yet reached her goal. It is hard to believe that she could have had at this early stage any premonition of the fame that Constant was later to acquire as a writer and statesman, but her quick intuition may well have led her to think his brilliant qualities might be an effective instrument in furthering her ambition. In spite of his profligate habits he was well educated and had a fertile and original mind. He was one of the few men she had ever met who could stand on her plane in conversation. And at the same time his admiration for her placed her in a position to dominate in all their intellectual encounters. That he had hitherto accomplished nothing only added to her zest. It is true that she once wrote, "All women crave a master. To make a woman really happy her love must look upwards." But she must have realized that she was an exception to the rule; she was never happy with a man she could not govern. And there never was a moment when she did not have Constant under her control.

In March, 1795, baron de Staël went to Paris, no longer an ambassador but with a commission from Sweden to collect the money his country had expended in the war between France and the Germanic powers. Two months later his wife again took up her abode in Paris, this time hoping to impress her personality upon the discordant elements which had emerged from the Revolution. Constant, it need scarce be said,

was with her. In the conflict of parties under the Directoire,
Germaine aspired to lead in bringing about a reconciliation.
She gathered about her a circle in which were found the most
irreconcilable elements. Every ten days she gave a dinner
at which all shades of opinion were represented, and on the
intervening days she entertained separately the leaders of
the various cliques. She was fast becoming the most popular
woman in Paris. Her old friend Talleyrand was there again
after his wanderings in America where he had set everybody
by the ears; and so was Montmorency whom she had snatched
from the guillotine. But along with these was Tallien, formerly a cook but now a member of the Directoire, and his
eccentric wife who tried to restore the dress of ancient Greece
among the gay women of the capital. It was a time when no
one could afford to be fastidious, and Germaine was the last
person to let her prejudices stand in the way of winning
popular favor. Only a year before, she had published certain
reflections on peace, in which she had hinted at a return of the
monarchy; and now she published her reflections on the trial
of the queen, in which she came out emphatically for a
republic, and in which all her former arguments in favor
of royalty were scattered to the winds.

To charge this impetuous young creature with insincerity
would not be altogether just. Her main fault was that in spite
of all her intellectual vigor her actions were generally
guided by her heart. It has often been said of her that she
argued one thing and did another. Judging her by her writings you would say she was a strict observer of the con-

ventionalities; yet she never seems to have had any qualms about ignoring convention in her private life. There was no correlation between her mental processes and her emotions. They belonged to two widely separated realms. While one was in action the other was at rest. In that way we can account for some of her inconsistencies. She honestly believed in the doctrine of equality which was the foundation stone of the republic, but when it came to obliterating class distinction her sentiments rebelled.

It was hardly to be expected that the people would understand. Soon they began to whisper that her intimacy with aristocrats had a sinister design. Almost without a warning she was ordered by the authorities to leave Paris. Her husband's effort in behalf of Sweden having come to naught, he returned to his native land and she retired to the suburbs of Paris. Her hope was that public sentiment would change, but instead of that it grew more bitter; and at last, realizing that the current had permanently set against her, she dropped her political aspirations and decided to employ her inexhaustible vitality on other things.

During all these years of political endeavor literary subjects had not been wholly absent from her thoughts. Full as her life had been with social and philanthropic duties she had never let her pen lie idle, though she had used it chiefly to disseminate her views on questions of government and administration. Her influence on those in charge of public matters having come to an end, she was now afforded opportunity in the quietude of Coppet to give more time to literary problems. The relish for works of fiction which had animated her youth had not been lessened by contact with the stern realities of life, and it was with feelings of intense enthusiasm that she fixed her thoughts once more upon the writers of romance.

One might be sure that in her studies of imaginative writing she would avoid the beaten track. A person of her temperament could never be happy except in exploring new fields, and in treating the subject of fiction she found occasion to present an idea which, if not entirely original, was at least different from that in current use. Now, to prescribe a set of rules to which writers of fiction must conform would be as futile as to insist on a uniform style of dress. The purpose of fiction is to interest and amuse. What pleases one generation bores another. Still, there will always be writers with vision to discern the popular trend before it has become pronounced; and of such writers Germaine certainly was one. She thought the fiction of her day inadequate and she set before herself the task of bringing about a change. As a preliminary step she offered to the public an Essai sur les fictions which brought into strong light some of those conceptions of imaginative writing which were destined later to make her famous. The fundamental idea was that fiction should be devoted first of all to the analysis of sentiment. She stressed the worthlessness of stories that were merely a record of incidents in the lives of individuals—that did not discuss the methods by which human feelings proceed to their final expression. In her view the finest specimen of fiction was

La nouvelle Héloïse. No novel, according to her, was worth reading which did not contain a lesson, which did not lead men to study their springs of action and the processes by which their sentiments were evolved.

The Essay on fiction was followed by a book on the influence of passion—a rather tiresome treatise along similar lines, important only because it shows that the author was formulating her thoughts as a preparation for imaginative work.

Then came another visit to Paris. "I would sooner," she says, "go before the revolutionary tribunal, where the chances of life and death are equal, than never return again to France." This time it was to relieve her husband who was overwhelmed with debts; and she brought him back to Coppet.

In the spring of 1797 she was in Paris again. Constant was ever at her side though he was at the same time paying devotions to Julia Talma, wife of the famous tragedian. Constant, as well as Talleyrand, was now hand and glove with the Directoire, while Germaine was out of favor. But she never let this stand in the way of her friendship with either of them. Talleyrand, in fact, was in financial straits and she advanced him money to put him on his feet, with the result that he was soon given the portfolio of foreign affairs. Constant was talked of for secretary of foreign affairs; but that plan fell through.

Napoleon had now become head of the army. His uninterrupted victories had made him the hero of the hour, and he was recognized everywhere as the greatest military genius of the world. Germaine was second to no one in her enthusiasm for him. She was present when her friend Talleyrand introduced him to the Directoire and she left no stone unturned to impress her personality upon him. From the very first interview, however, he resented her advances. She was not the type of woman that he admired. He could not endure a woman who was not submissive. He did not believe that women should meddle with politics. Her assertiveness and her habit of taking the leading part in conversation irritated and annoyed him. On one occasion when she was placed next to him at dinner she could hardly get him to open his mouth. It was not long after this interview that the Directoire decided to overthrow the government of Switzerland and make that country one of the departments of France. This task was entrusted to Napoleon and his military prowess enabled him to carry out the design. Germaine bitterly opposed the project, which she regarded as the enslavement of a liberty-loving people. She begged Napoleon not to strike this cruel blow, but he turned a deaf ear to her vehement appeal. As a result of this incident Napoleon made up his mind that she was an impediment to his ambition, and he resolved to spare no effort to destroy her influence.

About this time her husband permanently separated from her and she saw much more of Constant. Most of her friends disliked him; and some could not even tolerate his presence. He was now writing political pamphlets which everyone admitted were brilliant, but which many considered insin-

cere. One of her friends said that Constant "does all he can
to avoid being forgotten, but like a poisonous reptile he is
always causing pain. This is inherent in his nature, which is
impervious to softening influences." Even in her society he
was far from being serene. Whatever at the outset may have
been his feelings, it was not long before he chafed under
the domination of this absorbing woman. His pride revolted
against the submission of his individuality to another's will,
and yet he was so enthralled by the overpowering personality of Germaine that he could not give her up. Time and
again he resolved to bring their intimacy to a close, but it
always ended by his finding himself again at her feet. He
never was happy with her, and at the same time he was
miserable without her.

She was now passing her life alternately at Paris and at
Coppet. In 1798 she published her book, De la littérature.
Critics found this book too philosophical and declared she
twisted history to conform with her theories. But the book had
real value because it was the first serious effort to make the
French nation acquainted with the underlying characteristics
of German and English literature. Chateaubriand, who was
just coming into notice, thought this treatise filled with fanciful ideas and wrote her to that effect. Such criticism would
have irritated many writers, but it was characteristic of her
not easily to take offense. Two years later she met Chateaubriand and formed a friendship with him which lasted till
her death. Ultimately she and Chateaubriand found themselves working along the same lines. Together they did more

than any others to create the romantic school of literature in France.

The year 1800 brought Germaine once more into conflict with Napoleon. Aided by Talleyrand he had been appointed first consul, and a constitution had been framed establishing a senate and two chambers, to one of which Constant had been elected. One evening Germaine was entertaining at her house a number of men active in public life. Constant was among them; also Lucien Bonaparte, then minister of the interior. Constant was planning to speak the next day in opposition to certain proposals of the government, and he was urged by some of those present not to do so. Turning to Germaine, he asked her advice. She told him he must act according to his own convictions. The next day he made the speech, and before nightfall she received ten letters of regret from friends invited to dine with her that evening. One of these was from her old friend Talleyrand; and she never heard from him again. She still maintained her friendship with the family of the first consul, but Napoleon never forgave her for Constant's speech despite her vehement assertion that it was not inspired by her. The truth was, Napoleon could see nothing but evil in everything she did. In a letter to his brother he denounced Germaine for not helping her husband who was now financially ruined.

Germaine now gave up her handsome establishment in the rue de Bac and rented a modest house in the rue de Grenelle. She felt terribly depressed, but was somewhat consoled by an intimacy which she had formed with the lovely Jeanne

Récamier—an intimacy which ended only with Germaine's death. Germaine was not blind to the course that things were taking with Napoleon at the helm. He was rapidly becoming a dictator and all her hopes of liberty were crushed. It was clear enough he was waiting only for a favorable opportunity to drive her out of France. To avert this peril she refrained from giving further voice to her convictions but remained in Paris till the news was brought her that her husband was dying. She wrote at once that she would go to Sweden, to be at his side. That plan was changed. She persuaded him to go with her to Coppet, but he died suddenly on the way.

Napoleon wreaked his revenge on Constant by removing him from the chamber; and for the next twelve years Constant remained out of public life. Germaine and he were now inseparable. Neither of them could shake off the yoke, though both of them found it galling. In a letter to one of his friends Constant wrote, "Perhaps happiness is unattainable, as I cannot find it with the best and cleverest of women. How glad I should be to know that she is happy. My heart is too despondent, my soul is too fond of contradictions, my imagination is too discolored, for me to be able to give her happiness." On her part she was so restless, her emotions were so exalted, that she was kept in constant misery because it seemed as if her ideal of happiness never could be reached.

It was in this mood that she entered upon the composition of her first novel. Delphine, the heroine of the story, is a creature of impulse, who recognizes no criterion of conduct higher than her own conscience. She is generous, kindly, and self-sacrificing, but the impelling force which lies at the bottom of her nature and in the end outweighs every other impulse is a passionate and all-absorbing love. The author lets Delphine say, among other things, that she had never been loved so much as she had loved others, and that the strongest trait in her character was her capacity to suffer. One can see that Germaine was really describing her own emotions.

This book was eagerly read by Germaine's contemporaries. One critic who was not an admirer of the work admitted that the theaters were all empty because society preferred to stay at home and read Delphine. It was generally agreed that Germaine had produced an original story, though it was not at first realized that in attempting to make a careful analysis of emotions she had given birth to a new form of fiction which was soon to become exceedingly popular. To say that Delphine was a thoroughly artistic work would be going too far. Some of the characters do not seem altogether real. Here and there it is a little flamboyant, and the narrative is often interrupted by elaborate discussions on politics and philosophy. But on the whole the story is picturesque and entertaining.

Some critics objected to the writer's proneness to make light of marital relations. Undoubtedly when Germaine penned this novel her own experiences were surging through her brain. She puts into the mouth of Delphine's lover such arguments as came to her in excusing her own failure to adhere strictly to the marriage vows. But as the tale progresses she makes both the guilty parties suffer. The woman expiates her transgression in a cloister while her paramour goes into the army and is executed as a prisoner of war.

All this time Germaine was longing to go back to Paris, but Napoleon's brothers, whose friendship was as firm as ever, urged her not to go. As Napoleon grew in power he became more and more determined to brook no opposition and he made no secret of his unwillingness to tolerate her presence. She knew now that she could not lessen his animosity, but so deep was her affection for the capital that in the autumn of 1803 she ventured to rent a little house in the suburbs, hoping to stay there through the winter. She was hardly installed when it came to her ears that Napoleon had given orders that she must not remain in France. So she packed up her things and hurried to madame Récamier's country house, from which she wrote to Napoleon a pathetic letter begging him to allow her to stay at an estate her father owned on the outskirts of Paris. To this letter she received no answer, but a few days later officers arrived with a document signed by Napoleon forbidding her to come nearer than forty leagues from the capital. There was no escape from this peremptory order; and thus began a long period of sadness, the incidents of which she later set forth in her book, Dix ans d'exil.

Her thoughts were centered now on literary work, and she had grown enthusiastic about the romantic school of fiction which was already making progress among the German people. She was in deep sympathy with their aspirations and felt it would be a solace to her to live among them for a while and build up new ideals under the influence of their calmness and spirituality. So she started for Weimar, taking Constant with her. It was at this period that she wrote to a friend, "Benjamin is very good to me. I pray you to love him for the service that he renders me, and above all for the protection from evil that he affords me." She was unstrung by the severity of her punishment and found much comfort in Constant's presence.

She stayed all winter at Weimar, which was then the home of German culture. There she saw much of Goethe and Schiller. Her essays on literature had already given her an important place among the scholars of Germany, though the general feeling was that she lacked thoroughness in most of her work. Goethe had written that her book on fiction contained gleams of light rather than actual daylight. He found her clever, but biased. Schiller had discovered many beautiful thoughts in her writings, mingled with errors which he attributed to her sex. When she came into personal contact with these great men they could see that she was a most unusual person. She impressed them as a woman of extraordinary intellectual vigor, and they were electrified by her intense vitality. "The only defect in her," said Schiller, "is her overpowering volubility."

When Goethe wrote the story of his life he gave considerable space to her stay in Weimar. "Her presence had something charming about it both physically and mentally, and she did not appear to take it amiss if one appreciated both those qualities in her." She is known to have said, "I have never trusted a man who has not once been in love with me." She sometimes wearied Goethe, however, by her philosophical discussions. "She discussed conditions of thought and feeling that should be discussed only with God." And he remarked that she had no perception of what we call duty.

Constant seems to have been accepted as a matter of course in Weimar. It was noticed that she treated him as a younger brother, and, though he constantly argued with her, he was always respectful.

In the spring of 1804 she left Weimar and went to Berlin with letters of introduction from Joseph Bonaparte and was shown much attention by the Swedish ambassador. In that year Napoleon was crowned emperor and planned an attack on Prussia. It was natural that he should feel no friendship for a woman who was receiving so cordial a reception in Berlin. While there, she selected August Wilhelm von Schlegel, at Goethe's suggestion, as tutor for her boy.

She was in Berlin when her father died. It was a terrific blow to a woman with her sensitive feelings. Ten years later she wrote, "I owe gratitude on this earth only to God and to my father. My whole life has been a struggle; he alone blessed it. All that I acquired by my own efforts will vanish. My personal identity rests on the fidelity I maintain for his memory. I have loved those I no longer love, respected those I no longer respect. The waves of life have washed everything away except the great shadow on that mountain which points to the life that is to come."

Necker left her his whole fortune, amounting to three million francs beside the two million due from the French government. But money never meant anything to her except as a means to help others. During all the years of her exile she lived unostentatiously, though she gave lavishly to her friends. She once wrote to Schlegel to draw on her for anything he wanted and she would regard it merely as adding to their bond of friendship.

At the end of 1804 she went to Italy, fortified again with letters from Joseph Bonaparte. There she formed with Monti, the greatest contemporary Italian poet, an intimacy which was characteristic of her impulsive nature. She had known him only two weeks when she wrote him that his power of fascination had aroused her affection. All the time she was in Italy she kept up a correspondence with him couched in tender terms. "Love me," she says, "to such a degree that it costs you something to mention my name." On leaving Italy in June, 1805, she wrote to Monti, "It would have been less painful to me to take a personal farewell of you than bid farewell when the one to whom it is addressed is no longer present. It is like addressing prayers to an empty grave. I came here for your sake and now you have left me. I forgive you, but unconsciously you have broken my heart." And from Coppet she wrote him, "I have read the beginning of my Italian novel to my friends. They think it better than anything I have hitherto written. I know why." Such language seems a little strong, but must not be taken too seriously; she

once wrote to Goethe that she loved him and should admire
him as long as she lived.

The Italian novel to which she referred was Corinne, the
book on which her fame chiefly rests. Although she called it
her Italian novel, it was so only because Italy furnished the
setting. The hero was a puritanical Scotchman and the
heroine's father was an English lord. The psychology which
it portrays is wholly foreign to Italy. It is the psychology of
a talented, fascinating, enthusiastic, passionate daughter of
France—in short, the psychology of Germaine herself—and
by reason of that fact and that alone the book has great and
enduring value. Few women, and certainly no man, could
give us such a penetrating and in the main correct analysis
of all-possessing love. Only the intensity of her own emotions
enabled the authoress to do so. She was writing about the
force that was the mainspring of all she did. The public
accepted the book as her autobiography, and after its publication she was always called Corinne by those who knew her
best. Some of the passages in this book give us the best plum-
met we have to fathom the depths of her many-sided nature.

"You will perhaps want to know how much I should suffer
were you to forsake me. I know not. Sometimes there is
tumult in my soul; forces reign there more powerful than
my reason."

"Everything religious, even what is superstitious, has an
indescribable fascination for me, so long as it is tolerant and
free from enmity toward those who think differently.
As soon as our thoughts and sentiments rise above ordinary

things we need divine aid. Superior minds cannot do without it."

"In the happiness that he gave her there was no enduring guaranty. Perhaps that explains the intensity of her passion."

"Of what use are reproaches with regard to love? It would not be the tenderest and purest sentiment were it not the most spontaneous."

"Passionate natures betray themselves. That which is without bounds is without strength."

"Whilst striving for fame I always hoped that I should thereby attain love. What other use has a woman for fame?"

"Twice have I severed the bonds which fulfilled my heart's need and which I could not bring myself to make permanent."

This novel was received enthusiastically by the people and with more than ordinary praise by critics. Even Goethe, who was hard to please, said kind things about it. Byron remarked, "I knew madame de Staël well—better than she knows Italy—but I little thought I should one day think with her thoughts in the country where she has laid the scene of her most attractive production. She is sometimes right, and often wrong, about Italy and England; but almost always true in delineating the heart, which is of but one nation—of no country and yet of all." In attempting an accurate delineation of the heart she had blazed almost a new trail and was the forerunner of those romances which were so popular for the next fifty or sixty years.

Corinne, if we may now so call her, began the preparation of this book immediately after her return from Italy, but it was not published till two years later, in 1807, for she was busy through all this period in making strenuous efforts to get her decree of banishment removed. As emperor, Napoleon was determined to crush all opposition to his rule. Every step she took was watched and it was only with the greatest difficulty that she could secure a passport to enter France. Forbidden as she was to approach the capital she hired a house in the country where she was visited by Montmorency and other friends, and on four or five occasions she eluded the police and slipped into the capital, though she took care never to appear upon the streets till after dark. As soon as Napoleon was apprized he put the police upon her track, and to avoid arrest she had to go back to Coppet.

She was now the most celebrated woman in Europe, and her home became a center to which men of genius turned to gain new inspiration for literary work. She received them all with outstretched arms, and though her circle was often composed of somewhat incongruous elements her tact and gracious personality always smoothed things over. To keep her guests amused and perhaps to gratify her vanity she wrote some plays to be given in her salon. In these performances she as well as her guests took part. She was thus afforded opportunity to display her skill in depicting scenes of vehement emotion.

It was during this period that her intimacy with Constant reached its close. For some years Constant had been growing restive and had many times considered throwing off the yoke. In the spring of 1807 she received a letter from him

asking her to meet him at a little town near Geneva. Her
heart filled with misgivings, she hurried to the appointed
place only to be told that he was married. This was the end
of a liaison which had lasted thirteen years, and which in
spite of incessant wrangling neither of them had found it in
their hearts to break. Twice he had asked her to legalize
their intimacy but she had refused his offers, alleging that
she could not bring herself to change her name. The truth
was that her instinct told her she could never be happy as his
wife. His unstable character she knew would drive her mad.
Even while listening to his burning protestations she knew
there was no likelihood of permanency in his love. His gallantries were known to all the world, and though her ardent
nature drew her to him with a power she could not resist
there was always a consciousness that her ideal of happiness
was far beyond his reach. It may be that she demanded
more than it was in the power of any man to give. Of a cer-
tainty it required a stronger nature than Constant's to satisfy
the exigencies of her love. He tells us in his journal how she
was always lacerating his feelings even while he was under
the spell of her allurements. "I have bought a little dog," he
writes; "if he doesn't go mad I'm sure he will not bite me—
a thing I cannot say of some of my friends." Again and
again he declares he loves her more than any other woman in
the world and yet is worn out by her incessant pursuit of
distractions. When he was not with her he found no one to
make him happy. "All other people are nothing but trees
and rocks."

Sometimes when other women crossed his path he thought his love for Corinne was dead and he was irritated because she would not let him go. "I no longer love her; yet she will not be satisfied with mere friendship."

One evening when she was particularly depressed she upbraided him because he would not comfort her, and he made bold to tell her that she must find solace in herself, that it was nothing but a love of coquetry which made her dread old age, and nothing but vanity which made her always crave admiration. This language was brutal, but not altogether inexpressive of the truth.

On another occasion she forced him to sit up all night and listen to a discussion which she was having with Schlegel. Of course he obeyed but his journal contains this entry: "I have never seen a better woman nor one with more grace and devotion. At the same time I have never seen a woman whose exigencies, without her being conscious of it, are more continuous, who absorbs more of the lives of those about her. . . . Every minute of their existence must be at her disposal. And when she gives way to fury she is like a hurricane or an earthquake."

A few days later he writes in desperation: "I have told her two hundred times that our love is over. I must detach my life from hers, either by remaining simply a friend or by disappearing from the world."

And again: "Dined with Bonstetten, Schlegel, and Sismondi like schoolboys when the regent is away. Strange woman! Her domination over everyone about her is inexplicable, though real. If she knew how to govern herself she could govern the whole world."

Another evening Minette, as he sometimes called her, was in bad humor because he wouldn't sit up. "It is clear I've got to marry, so as to go to bed early."

Pretty soon he regrets his harshness. "How can I have the heart to cool the affection of a woman whom I love so deeply and rob her of her last friend just as she has lost her father?" She had tickled his vanity by praising one of his writings. "Still, she has such a tendency to emotion that her praise doesn't prove the beauty of the piece."

He was greatly relieved when she decided to go to Italy, but she wearied him by her elaborate preparations. On the way she stopped at Lyon, where her friend Camille Jordan lived. Jordan was a brilliant writer, for whom Corinne entertained more than an intellectual regard, and Constant in a fit of jealousy followed her to that city. She had asked Jordan to go to Italy with her. His refusal to do so served to calm Constant and he left her and went to Paris. There he wrote her a batch of mournful letters—so sad in fact that she begged him to let her know what she could do for him. "Alas," he wrote in his journal, "what I want is my liberty, and that she won't let me have."

"I have received a very nice letter from madame de Staël. She is always in too much of a hurry to push herself ahead. Agitation and ambition. She leaves the wings of fortune no time to grow. She is always plucking out the feathers to make herself a plume. . . . Women are all egotists. They sacrifice everything to gratify a momentary fancy. And yet how hard it is to resist them!"

"Madame de Staël is enchanted by her success in Rome. What a pity that she is so ambitious for these little successes that cost her so much effort!"

"I am worn out with these incessant reproaches and my incessant justification. When a woman is in love, nothing but love will satisfy her."

He had sworn that he would never go back to Coppet, but after her return from Italy we find him there again.

In the following year, 1806, after Corinne had taken a house at Auxerre, she wrote to him to come to her. He characterized her letter as a convulsion of the universe. "However, with all her faults she is more than all others to me," and he obeyed again, only to give rise to more recriminations.

Then again to Coppet after her flight from Auxerre. "Madame de Staël has reconquered me." But it was only for a moment. "Her impetuosity and self-assertion are a torment and perpetual danger to me. I must break with her if possible. It is the only way for me to lead a tranquil life."

The next year, 1807, she was attending to the publication of Corinne and he was in Paris trying to get the ban against her removed. But his thoughts were now taken up with the lady whom he was to marry. He tried to keep this a secret, but Corinne got wind of what was going on and pursued him, "foaming at the mouth and with a poniard in her hand." She threatened to kill herself if he abandoned her. So he went back to Coppet and things continued in the same way for two or three years more until finally he shook off the chains and married the woman who would give him, as he thought, repose.

Two years later, which years had passed without her seeing him, she wrote, "I never take out my writing materials without picking up your letters and looking at your handwriting on the envelopes. All I have suffered through that handwriting makes me shudder, and yet I would fain see it again." Her wish was gratified. Before her death she was able to help him in the political career on which he was about to embark. But the intimacy which for thirteen years had held them together was cherished only as a memory of the past.

To assuage her grief she now turned her thoughts upon the work on Germany which had long been taking shape in her brain. This book cost her more effort than any other of her writings. It did more even than Corinne to place her on a pedestal as an international celebrity. Her banishment from France had driven her into communion with the intellectual leaders of Germany, and had brought her gradually to feel intense enthusiasm for the fundamentals of German thought. She loved the spontaneity of the people and the frank and natural way in which they voiced their feelings. German literature seemed to her to have its foundation in the realities of life. To set forth these conceptions was the main purpose of her book. When it appeared some people criticized her for giving too much space to unimportant matters, for philosophizing about things which she did not wholly understand, and for adopting a style of argument which was too vehement and impassioned for so sedate a theme; but on the whole the verdict was that her book on Germany was bound to exert an important influence on the literature of her time.

Though still forbidden to set her foot on the soil of France, she was determined to seek a publisher in Paris. It was a foolhardy thing to do. Apart from Napoleon's determination to keep her in the background, the book was sure to rouse his ire. There was nothing in it which he could take as a personal affront, but it was a candid effort to idealize the nation with which he was at war. Anyone but Corinne could have predicted that he was bound to take offense. With the same disregard of consequences which she showed in all her acts, she sent her manuscript to the publisher who had printed Corinne and went herself to a place just forty leagues from Paris to superintend the revision of the proofs; but before the book was issued the chief of police seized all the copies that had been printed and again she was ordered out of France. This was in 1810, and the book was not published in Paris till after the emperor's abdication.

On her return to Coppet she was watched more closely than ever. She was virtually a prisoner, forbidden to travel more than ten miles from her home. What distressed her most was that she was denied the society of her friends. Some avoided her as they would the pest, fearing to incur the emperor's wrath if they had anything to do with her. A few were actually exiled from France because ney had the hardihood to visit her at Coppet. A deep gu.f stood between her and all she held most dear. Even a harmless book review which she wrote for one of the French journals was returned to her by the publisher, as no one dared to print anything from her pen. She was in constant anxiety lest her three children be placed under the ban, and at one time actually made arrangements to migrate to the United States in order to escape persecution.

The emperor's marriage with Marie Louise of Austria was the signal for many acts of clemency and Corinne asked the Austrian ambassador to use this as a pretext for terminating her exile, but Napoleon was adamant. "I will not have her in Paris," he replied. Whereupon she wrote him a pathetic and most humble letter in which she said that the eight years of exile which she had already endured had taught her humility. She begged him to allow her to return that she might have her children brought up in Paris. To this appeal the emperor made no reply.

Then came what was perhaps the most curious episode in the life of this emotional woman. There was living in Geneva a young man named Rocca, who had been seriously wounded while fighting in the French army. When still an invalid he had become infatuated by the amazing vitality of Corinne who was more than twenty years his senior, and she had invited him to come to Coppet, at that period almost deserted. The friends on whom she had always counted were there no more. Unutterably lonely, she felt that she was beaten down by conditions in the face of which she had no power to rise. All the fame and glory which she had enjoyed seemed to have brought her little happiness and to have ended in despair. She had reached the autumn of life and in looking back she could see that all the romances of her existence had brought no satisfaction. She had charmed and fascinated people by the brilliancy of her thoughts and the fluency of her conversation, but she had to confess that she had never inspired what above all else she craved—a sincere, unshakeable love. When Rocca came into her life he seemed to embody the image of everything she had dreamed. His adoration fanned into life again her ambition to do great things. His frailty, his eagerness to shelter himself under her protecting wings, filled her with pride. His youth, his deference to her ever-changing wishes, his gentleness and unobtrusiveness touched her heart and re-awakened in her the dormant passion of her youth.

Corinne's intimacy with Rocca brought her nearer to the fulfillment of her desires than any other of her loves. All her other romances had been wrecked by the clashing of discordant ambitions. Narbonne and Constant, and all who had hitherto succumbed to the fascination of this singular woman, had been men of too strong individuality to yield themselves completely to her power. But Rocca's individuality was swallowed up in hers. She took him into her arms as a mother takes her child. She watched over him with a tenderness which her tempestuous nature had not before revealed, and to the end of her life she remained steadfast in her devotion to this fragile youth.

Meantime the emperor was tightening his grip on Germany, and Corinne began to fear his soldiers would descend on Coppet. She determined to flee before it was too late. As the widow of de Staël it seemed to her she would be safe in Sweden, but, since Napoleon's troops were scattered all over Germany, the only method of reaching her destination was through Russia. On the 23rd of May, 1811, in company with Rocca, she started on the perilous journey, leaving in Coppet their only child who had been born three months before. Her way led through Austria which held aloof while Napoleon was planning his attack on Moscow, and in Vienna she received a passport allowing her to enter Russia. The strain of the last few years had worked havoc with Corinne's constitution and a journey by carriage for fifteen hundred miles over ill constructed roads was no light task; but she was not the one to turn back, and in the dreadful winter of 1812, in which Napoleon's shattered army retreated from Moscow, she made her way to Stockholm. In the following June, after one of her sons had been killed in a duel, she forsook Stockholm and took up her abode in London. There she published the first edition of her book on Germany. It was received with great enthusiasm and brought her into close touch with all the literary people of the day. Byron, who had known her in happier days, found her sadly changed. "Her works are my delight," he says, "and so is she herself—for half an hour." She tired him with her long speeches and he charged her with being vain; but "who," he adds, "had an excuse for vanity if she had not?" Mary Berry, the writer, remarked that if one wanted to see the crown ministers he must go to madame de Staël's house, for they were always there. Wilberforce after dining with her one evening declared, "The whole scene was intoxicating even to me. The fever arising from it is not yet gone."

In spite of all this adulation she was far from happy. Rocca, though always devoted, lacked the intellectual qualities which she needed for real companionship and his constant presence kept closed some doors which she would have been glad to enter. She could not wholly banish Constant from her thoughts, and one day on receiving a letter from him, she replied, "To see you once again would be to revive my spirit and give me hope which with all else seems to be gone forever. If you do not come here, I shall go to the continent . . . Benjamin, you have destroyed my life. For ten years no day has gone by without my suffering on your account. How I have loved you! But let that pass—it is too cruel. Yet I shall never be able to forgive you, for I shall never cease to suffer."

The fall of Napoleon in 1814 came to her as a shock. Deeply as she resented his persecution of her, she grieved for the disaster that had overwhelmed France. Constant, who was now in the thick of politics, sent her a pamphlet which called forth a reply. "How much," she wrote, "I would wish to talk over this, but where is the subject I should not wish to discuss with you? Intellectually at least we shall always sympathize with each other . . . I shall carefully and zealously guard your interests. Write to me. I have not ceased and shall not cease writing to you. You have brought me much harm, and the longer I live here the more clearly I see that your character is unworthy. But I respect your talent and the sentiment which filled my heart for so many years. I shall always remain your friend."

As soon as Napoleon was taken to Elba, Corinne returned to Paris and her house became once more a gathering-place of celebrated men. Among the notables whom she received were the emperor of Austria, the ambassadors of all the foreign powers, La Fayette, and her old friend Montmorency. Louis XVIII had been raised to the throne, but there was bitter strife among the publicists as to the nature of his rights. Corinne took the side of those who claimed that France was now a constitutional monarchy, and by so doing clashed with Constant who had become the leading champion of the doctrine of hereditary succession. Corinne, though in shattered health, could not keep out of the fray. The Duke of Wellington, who saw her at this time, said he wished he could keep her out of politics. "I have told her more than once," he wrote, "that I hated to talk politics, and she replied that politics was her life. She and I were great friends." This was but one more illustration of her power to fascinate. Through all her life she had statesmen and scholars at her feet. Many of them abhorred her politics and grew restive under the constant exhibition of her egotism, but rare indeed was the man who did not sooner or later succumb to the charm of her warm and sympathetic nature.

The genuineness of her emotions is manifest in her deep affection for madame Récamier, the famous beauty who broke so many hearts among the potentates of Europe. Their acquaintance began in a business transaction, and madame Récamier has left us a record of her first impression of her celebrated friend. "I was struck by the beauty of her eyes. . . . She fixed her great eyes upon me, with a curiosity mingled with kindliness. . . . From that day, I could think of nothing but her, so deep an impression had been made on me by her ardent and forceful nature." Madame Récamier was then only twenty-one, but her dazzling beauty and her position as the wife of a rich banker had already brought her to the front of social life in Paris. So she and Corinne met frequently, and their friendship was cemented by the intimacy which they both enjoyed with Montmorency. Ever since Corinne had rescued him from the guillotine he had remained her stanchest friend, and his unselfish attachment to these two women was always a bond which held them close together. When Napoleon came into power he was attracted, as was everybody else, by madame Récamier's marvellous beauty, but he grew irritated with her as soon as he found she did not respond to his advances. All his ministers were paying court to madame Récamier and on one occasion he asked them petulantly if they held their state council at her house. His enmity toward madame Récamier did much to cement her friendship with Corinne. When Corinne was exiled, madame Récamier's first thought was to shelter her friend, and it was to her house that Corinne fled as soon as the order of exile was signed. In commenting on that catastrophe madame Récamier used words which show how deep their affection for each other had become. "I admire madame de Staël passionately. This arbitrary and cruel act which has separated her from me is despotism in its most odious form. A man who could banish such a woman and be the cause of such unhappiness can be, to my way of thinking, naught but a pitiless despot."

Two years later madame Récamier told Napoleon's minister of police that she had lost all respect for his master on account of the persecution of Corinne.

Not long after, it came to be Corinne's turn to offer consolation to her beautiful young friend. Récamier's bank failed, and his wife was left with nothing except a small income from her mother. "Oh! my dear Juliette," wrote Corinne, "what a grief I feel at this awful news! How I curse this exile which prevents my being near you and pressing you to my heart! . . . May I not cherish the dream of seeing you here this winter? Come for three months to my narrow circle where you will be passionately cared for. If not that, then I shall go to my forty leagues from Paris to see you, to throw my arms around you and tell you that I hold you dearer than any other woman I have ever known. . . . Dear Juliette, let our friendship grow stronger than ever, let it not be merely acts of kindness on your part, let it be an unbroken correspondence, a need of confiding our thoughts to each other, a life together."

Juliette, as Corinne called her, could not accept Corinne's invitation at once but in the summer of 1807 she went to Coppet and remained three months. After she had gone, Corinne went to Vienna, where she spent the winter of 1808. On her return she set to work vigorously on her book on Germany and for two years scarcely ever left Coppet, but Juliette frequently visited her there and took part in the plays which her talented hostess had written.

In the summer of 1810 Corinne took a house near Blois for three months. "My dear Juliette," she wrote, "my heart beats with pleasure at the thought of seeing you. Arrange to give me all the time you can." Juliette came and for several weeks Corinne had all her dearest friends about her. Montmorency and Constant were, of course, among them. To amuse her guests she originated what she called her petite poste. They all sat around a table and wrote letters to one another. One of Corinne's letters has been preserved. It reads thus: "Dear Juliette, your visit is drawing to a close. I can conceive no country and no inner life without you. I realize there are some emotions which seem to be necessary for me, but I know also that everything will fall away when you depart. You are the sweet and tranquil center of our life here and it is by you alone that we are all held together. God grant that this summer may return."

Juliette had scarcely gone when Corinne learned that her book had been seized by the authorities, and she was given peremptory orders to depart from France at once. Corinne wrote to Juliette, "Dear friend, I am overwhelmed with grief . . . you, dear angel, who have loved me for my misfortune, who have never known me but in adversity, and who have always been so sweet to me, you also I must lose."

Juliette went to her friend queen Hortense and begged her to intercede with Napoleon, and she also made a personal appeal to the censor, but without result.

When Corinne imparted to her friend that she was planning to escape from Coppet, Juliette could not bear to let her go without a final visit. Montmorency had just been exiled for visiting Corinne, and Juliette was cautioned lest a like fate befall her. She paid no heed beyond letting it be publicly known that she was going to Aix. She remained with Corinne only thirty-six hours, and on her way back to Paris learned that she, too, had been exiled. She did not see Paris again until Napoleon had left the throne.

Corinne's first duty when she returned to Paris in the spring of 1814 was to send this message to Juliette: "I am ashamed to be in Paris without you, dear angel of my life. I must know your plans. May I see you at Coppet where I am going to spend four months?" This never came about, but a few days later Juliette after three years of absence returned to Paris, and the bonds of friendship between these two devoted women became firmer than ever. Napoleon's implacable hostility had blighted both their lives and together they now sought to efface the bitter memories of their persecution. As victims of the fallen despot they were cajoled and flattered as they had never been before.

In the midst of this rejoicing Corinne had to endure one

more cruel blow. Constant, ever ready for some new enchant-
ment, developed a mad infatuation for Corinne's dearest
friend. As Juliette never gave the slightest indication of
reciprocating his love, this brutal disregard of Corinne's
feelings is hardly worthy of comment, except so far as it
furnishes proof of Corinne's loyalty to the man she once had
loved. Humiliating as the position was in which he placed
her, she uttered no reproach. Whatever suffering he might
cause her she had steeled her heart to bear.

The fact was, her troubled life was drawing to a close.
Her thoughts were turning toward the past, and she was busy
with what was to be her final work, the Considérations sur la
révolution française. That work shows on every page that she
was coming to take a calmer view of life. She realized that
the liberty which she dreamed about was hardly attainable
under either an emperor or a king. The evils that had come
on France were not due wholly to those in power. The people
were largely to blame. "They do not know what liberty
means." Such thoughts as these were not in harmony with
the sentiments of her friends, and she absented herself more
and more from Paris. Juliette begged her to come back from
Coppet, and she replied, "No, indeed, I could not be thank-
ful for the liberty guaranteed. Being of the opinion that
nations are born free, I should let fall words that are not
in fashion and should only make enemies for myself."

On the pretext of nursing Rocca, she spent the winter of
1816 in Italy, and while there she gave her daughter in mar-

riage to the duc de Broglie, a scion of one of the most aristocratic families in France. Constant had now thoroughly
passed out of her life and he learned of this event only in a
roundabout way. He wrote to Juliette that he knew Broglie
but did not feel it incumbent on him to congratulate Corinne.
"I do not think she has need of an excessive tenderness. By
the overflow of her own feelings and the unavoidable reaction
in her own nature, she has brought up sensible children."

The sojourn in Italy had done Rocca good. In a letter to
Juliette, Corinne wrote what a comfort he was to her. "Such
patience, such thorough appreciation of and thankfulness
for my care, have made him the most perfect friend that I
can imagine."

Winter over, she returned to Coppet and Juliette paid her
a visit, as did also Lord Byron. In writing of her at this time
Byron remarked, "She is the best creature in the world."

This was very nearly the end. Once more she came to
Paris, and tried to renew her active association with her
friends. But it was no use. At a large dinner party at a
friend's house she fainted and had to be carried home. This
was her last appearance in public. In the few months that
remained to her of life, the asperity which had often annoyed
her friends passed entirely away, though she did not seem
to realize the change that had come over her. She said to
Chateaubriand who came to see her, "In joy or sorrow I
have always been the same. I have loved God, my father, and
liberty." On the evening before her death the faithful Mont-

morency called, and she asked him to see if Rocca had taken his medicine.

The end came on the fourteenth of July, 1817. Her remains were carried to Coppet, and it is gratifying to note that Constant was one of those who accompanied her body to the grave.

DELPHINE GAY

In THE early part of the nineteenth century one could lay no claim to special distinction merely on the ground that he was a writer. In one way or another almost every man of political or social importance dabbled with the pen. Some of the leading statesmen, like Lamartine and Victor Hugo, were poets or novelists; others, like Thiers, became distinguished writers of history. Chateaubriand, nominally a diplomatist, owes his reputation chiefly to his treatises on philosophical subjects. Never before had France produced so brilliant and versatile a galaxy of authors. And the most notable fact about this profusion of literary endeavor was that it covered almost every field of intellectual activity. It was a period of mental and material expansion, fairly illustrated in the personality of Delphine Gay.

WHEN Lamartine, the poet-statesman, was visiting the ruins of Terni in 1825, he caught sight of a young woman who appealed to his romantic spirit as the most beauteous creature he had ever seen. Delphine Gay, the object of his adoration, was then just twenty-one, and she had already become a center of admiration in Paris not only because of her statuesque beauty but on account of her talent as a composer of delicate and graceful verse. Her mother, Sophie Gay, was a novelist of some repute whose salon was frequented by all the literary men. This may account, in part,

DELPHINE GAY

for the enthusiasm with which the daughter's youthful effusions were acclaimed; but, whatever the reason, it was the general opinion that Delphine was destined to become one of the leading poetesses of the period.

As the years went on, she did not from a literary point of view justify altogether the prophesies of her early admirers. But her personal charm, and the serenity and joyousness of her nature, came in time to draw into her sphere of influence all the intellectual geniuses of her day. Lamartine, Victor Hugo, Chateaubriand, Eugene Sue, Gautier, Balzac, Alfred de Musset, and George Sand owed much of their inspiration to the hours they spent with this fascinating and gifted woman who presided over "the house with the marble columns" in the rue de Chaillot in Paris.

Whether under favoring circumstances her skill in versification might have led her ultimately to take high rank among the poets cannot now be proved. Some of her best verses were written after she matured. But on marrying Émile de Girardin her thoughts were diverted into less pretentious channels, and for about twelve years she employed her talent chiefly in writing prose. Girardin was the founder and editor of La Presse, a journal which became in time the leader of public opinion, and from 1836 till the fall of Louis-Philippe there appeared at intervals in that journal, under the caption of the Courrier de Paris, a series of articles on social and political problems bearing the signature of vicomte Charles de Launay. Only those who were in close touch with the newspaper's administration were aware that

Charles de Launay was the beautiful and accomplished wife of Émile de Girardin.

It is in these articles, later published under the title of Lettres parisiennes, that we are enabled best to get at Delphine's mental processes and to understand why she was so genuinely worshipped by all the distinguished writers of her time. Viewed as literary compositions these articles certainly do not have exceptional merit. Perhaps that would be more than we should have a right to expect in work so largely dependent on the exigencies of the press. It must be borne in mind, moreover, that as a contributor to a popular journal the writer was bound to cater to many tastes and it would not do for her to follow definite lines of thought so fully as to bring her arguments always to a cogent end. There was one thing, however, that she was always permitted, if not required, to do, namely, to amuse; and in that field she was entirely at her ease. Her leading characteristic was a love of mirth. Lamartine, who in spite of his affection for her was always a little petulant, once told her he wished she would try to restrain her incessant laughter. It may be that this trait hindered her progress in writing poetry, but unquestionably her inexhaustible humor and her keen enjoyment of the amusing experiences of those about her were responsible in large measure for the popularity of her Lettres parisiennes.

She never tired of making merry over the foibles of humanity and it gave her delight to find a basis for men's folly in fundamental traits. She loved to divide men into classes and to show that each class had its special characteristics. There were the dog-men, kind, brave, faithful, honest, but credulous and improvident. Then there were the cat-men, egotistical, avaricious, jealous, perfidious, but adroit, intelligent, and capable. Examples of dog-men were Socrates, Regulus, Washington. Among cat-men she enumerated Ulysses, Hannibal, Pericles, Richelieu. Sometimes it was a little difficult to determine to which class a man really belonged. By association with the other class one's traits were more or less modified, and that was always a source of danger because the acquired traits were never thoroughly sincere. Napoleon, a cat-man by nature, dreamed of vengeance, but he discarded his dream of vengeance only to dream of glory.

In like vein is her letter on taking up the carpets, the most dreaded event of the whole year. "The air is full of dust. A horrible pounding has been going on all the morning, and now a heavy rumbling sound pervades the house. The atmosphere is thick with the smell of soap-suds. You sit in a room as bare as a desert. Before your eyes a number of fat, half-clad workmen are carrying off all your precious relics . . . Not a room in the whole apartment is habitable. One room has been entirely stripped, and in another your furniture is packed up to the ceiling. Chairs are piled up on the tables, and the sofa cushions are in heaps upon the chairs. You try to open your desk which is behind a mountain of furniture, and you find the cover held down by a corner of the piano. Happy is the man who can slip off to the country when they come to take up his carpets."

Then we have a description of the "fictitious absence" which was common in Paris and not entirely unknown in other capitals. When summer comes, fashion decrees that you must get out of Paris. Some go to their country estates, some to the watering places, some take long trips. People of self-respect cannot remain in the city, lest they be thought grocers or journalists, or ministers or porters. But to go to your country place you must have a country place; to travel you must have money in your pocket. So some people cannot travel. But they can always bid their friends "good-by." You can stay in Paris if you don't let people see you. It's easy enough. You pull down the blinds, and instruct the porter to say you are out of town. You shut yourself up with your wife in a room at the back of the court. You stay there three months while you are travelling. Each night at twelve you offer your arm to your travelling-companion and saunter through the streets. At the end of the summer you reappear in the capital, a little fatigued by your journey, but enchanted, rich in souvenirs—and not at all sunburned. You may not have had much amusement, but you have kept your reputation as a person of fashion, and you can remark to those whose business has chained them here, "I don't see how anyone can spend the summer in Paris."

And so she runs on with amusing descriptions of public ceremonies and domestic complications, interspersed with extremely learned dissertations on dresses, and women's hats and handkerchiefs, on the pictures in the Salon, on the famous balls, the open-air festivities, with criticisms of the latest books and theatrical performances—with everything, in fact, that goes to make up the daily life of a bustling people struggling to outstrip one another in the race for social recognition.

As a journalist she had to keep abreast of the times and record all the events which interested her readers. But by reading between the lines, you can often detect that her thought is deeper than her expression. The French, she says, are accused of being flippant. That is not so, she declares. They are light of heart, but not of character. "They can die with a smile on their lips and that is proof of a sublime philosophy."

In spite of her eagerness to avoid a jar, she did occasionally venture to castigate some of the practices that were prevalent among her readers. Drawing a lesson probably from her own bringing-up, she was utterly opposed to the manner in which most children were educated. Education, she says, has now become so systematized that a child can learn to read in fifteen days and to count in three weeks. In her view such a system took no account of the main purpose in training children, namely, to make them think. No permanent benefit can be obtained except through effort. "One soon forgets what he has learned, but he never forgets what he has found out." That was a sound doctrine which could hardly give offense.

A little more risky was her reply to someone who said men's clubs were ruining society. No, she says, the clubs have merely absorbed those who were uncomfortable in society—in other words, the bores. That Delphine should have dared to publish so sweeping an indictment of her fellow-citizens shows how strong a hold she had on their affections. She had almost gained the prerogative of a jester whose buffoonery can not offend. No one was exempt, or expected to be exempt, from her genial pleasantry. She tells her readers she prefers the homœopathic to the allopathic doctor—it is better to have one who lets you die than to have one who gives you medicines that kill.

Here is another comment which might well cause her readers to reflect: "People do not want the truth. A mirror which shows them as they are would horrify them."

And what would the fair sex say to this? "A woman's whole life is ambition. To be important is her dream. Love, to a woman, means nothing but success. She wishes to be loved only to assure herself that she is lovable."

It is not often that Delphine discourses on religion, though there are reasons to believe it was not always absent from her thoughts. In one passage she says, "With people who have no faith, publicity takes the place of confession. . . . Morality exists only for those who have it not. Those who are moral never speak of it. They take it as a matter of course."

The corner-stone of her religion was joy. Through all the ages, she tells us, happiness has been thought of as a precious stone which men are always seeking but have never found.

Far from that is the truth. Happiness is a mosaic of thousands of little stones, valueless by themselves, but, when joined together, of transcendent beauty.

This may seem like poetry, and in truth her way of looking at everything was poetic. Describing the orangerie in the Luxembourg gardens she says God must have wanted to punish the French people when he forbade the superb pineapple to ripen in Paris. And in placing the strawberry so close to the ground, and making it so delicate to the touch, he must have intended that it should be plucked only by the tiny hands of children.

In one of her letters she gives us her conception of "the true woman"—a little fanciful, perhaps, but still indicative of discernment. "She is a frail creature, ignorant, timid, and indolent, who cannot live by herself, who loses color at a cross word and blushes at a kind one, whose life is guided by an inspiration from above—an inexplicable being with noble qualities in big things and amiable defects in little ones. She is a treasure-house of fears and hopes."

Delphine certainly would not have cared for the modern woman. A woman's duty, she says, is to reign, not govern. Men do not want women to share their work but to distract them from it. Her ideal woman was the famous tragédienne Rachel, who began life as a street singer and ended with the reputation of being the most artistic actress that the world had ever known. To Delphine more than to any other person Rachel owed her early recognition by the theater-goers of Paris. She was but seventeen when the Lettres parisiennes began to sing her praises, and in less than two years after Delphine had become her sponsor Rachel's genius was proclaimed on every hand. Soon after, an intimacy grew up between these women which had an important influence upon the lives of both.

To get a clear picture of the situation one must know a little about the current of French dramatic art. Ever since madame de Staël had published her epoch-making novels there had been a growing interest in romance—that is to say, in books which portrayed the development of personality instead of furnishing a mere recital of events. Readers were breaking away from the classics and the so-called romantic school was getting the upper hand. Under the leadership of Lamartine, and Alfred de Musset, and Alfred de Vigny, and Victor Hugo, stories that depicted contemporary emotions were the only things anybody cared to read. The smaller theaters in Paris yielded gradually to the popular taste, and in 1830 the Comédie-Française so far acquiesced as to permit Victor Hugo's Hernani to be produced. The success of this performance was so emphatic that the romantic writers were confident they had won the day. But the Comédie-Française was a national institution and was not yet ready to give up the fight. That was the situation when Rachel accepted a contract from the national theater, and her marvellous powers as a tragédienne went far to restore the popularity of the classics. Her acting of Racine's Phèdre won so universal applause that for the time being the romanticists were hushed.

Delphine, whose idealism led her to glorify the splendors of the past, threw all her influence in favor of the classics, and conceived the project of writing a tragedy to be played by Rachel. It was a play in which Rachel, by reason of her hebraic ancestry, seemed eminently fitted to play the leading rôle. She seems to have entered into the scheme with enthusiasm, and to have encouraged Delphine to go on with the work. She writes, "I dream of Judith and of its author. Our talk together comes often to my memory, and I hope you will finish what you have so well begun. You are good enough to ask me to encourage you in your desire that I should play the rôle. Did I not know your modesty, I should reply that it would fill me with pride to do so." The play was given at the Comédie-Française in 1843, and was vociferously applauded, as all of Rachel's acting was, and four years later another of Delphine's tragedies, Cléopâtre, was presented on the same stage with Rachel once more in the title rôle. This was Delphine's final effort as a writer of tragic plays. In spite of the artistic acting of the great tragédienne it was manifest that the plays themselves did not rise above mediocrity. Tragic drama was entirely outside the realm of Delphine's talent.

Meantime the success of her Lettres parisiennes had brought Delphine to realize that by confining herself to comedy she was more likely to excel. Her first production in that line, C'est la faute du mari was a rather unpretentious piece. This was followed in 1853 by Lady Tartuffe, in which she succeeded in persuading Rachel to take the leading part.

This comedy, though not a work of genius, was much better than anything else that Delphine wrote for the stage. The name, of course, was borrowed from Molière's famous play in which Tartuffe was represented as a sanctimonious hypocrite who shrank from no duplicity to gain his selfish ends. Delphine, in selecting Lady Tartuffe as the central figure of her comedy, undertook to show that hypocrisy was not confined exclusively to the ruder sex. Some of the situations which she depicts are not altogether real. The shifting of sentiment is altogether too swift and outruns the recital of events which most persons would require in order to recast their views. The strength of the piece lies in the writer's skill in developing a mystery. Until the curtain is about to fall in the last act you cannot determine exactly where to place the guilt. Lady Tartuffe, a penurious widow whose marriage certificate appears to be more or less mythical, wants to marry a rich old marquis, whose thoughts are too busy with the approaching marriage of his favorite niece to let his mind be turned to the question of a matrimonial alliance for himself. Lady Tartuffe has an interview with the marquis and tells him of a serious indiscretion which the young niece had committed a short time before at the marquis' country estate, and the recital of this event so horrifies the marquis that he resolves to disown his entire family. Lady Tartuffe by her activity in sponsoring philanthropies has gained the reputation of a paragon of virtue, and the marquis, overwhelmed with gratitude for her disinterested labor in disclosing to him the truth, asks her to become his wife. The young girl's fiancé, who, as it turns out, had once been Lady Tartuffe's lover, and hence is familiar with her duplicity, demands that she produce her proofs. The gardener on the marquis' estate is therefore summoned. Though heartbroken at having to recount a story so damaging to his employer's family, he divulges the whole affair. He was sound asleep, he says, when he was awakened about three o'clock in the morning by the barking of his dog. He jumped out of bed and, seizing his gun, rushed out on the lawn to see what was the matter. He hid behind one of the bushes and saw mademoiselle all in white in the center pathway which was under the full light of the moon. He noticed that she was not alone. She seemed perfectly calm though she appeared anxious not to be seen. There was a young man with her and she was evidently on very familiar terms with him. She huddled close up to him in a caressing sort of way. When they reached the garden gate the gardener climbed up on the wall to see who the young man was, and then he saw that it was Charles Valleray, son of the prefect, whom the family had refused to receive in their home because of his political views. Just then he heard a window being closed in the hôtel de France, which adjourned the château; and the whole incident caused him such distress that he asked the family to let him leave their service, hoping thus to avoid being questioned about his mistress's young daughter to whom he had been devotedly attached ever since she was a child.

This straightforward recital seemed to leave no doubt

about the young girl's guilt. Even her mother was forced to admit it. No one dared to stand up for her except her fiancé, who demanded that she be summoned and explain her conduct if she could. And this is what she said:

"My mother had been dangerously ill—oh! so ill, for three weeks. She no longer recognized us. Her great eyes stared straight ahead but saw nothing. We all despaired of her life. They all looked at me and whispered 'poor child.' It was terrible. At last toward evening of that day she grew calmer, and the doctor said if she could sleep three or four hours she would recover. Then he left and soon after mamma fell into a gentle sleep. Without saying a word, almost without breathing, old Thérèse and Fanny and I made preparations for the night. Thérèse curled herself up in a big armchair, Fanny went to sleep in her bed, and I fell on my knees in prayer. The silence was so deep that I could hear the clock tick, and the idea came to me to creep up to it and stop it so that it would not strike and wake mamma. I had no sooner done that than I heard at the end of the garden our big watchdog Caesar barking as if he were mad, and he kept coming nearer to the house, barking louder and louder. Oh! my God! I thought, if he should come and bark under mamma's windows he would wake her and all the benefit of her sleep would be lost. Hardly conscious of what I did I seized a little lamp which was on the table and ran downstairs. 'Perhaps it is robbers,' I said to myself, but I felt no fear. I was full of courage. I opened the front door and what did I see on the terrace? This rabid Caesar in the act of tearing to pieces a young man. While Caesar had his teeth on the young man there was no danger, for he couldn't bark. But the young man had in his hand a stout stick with which he was striking at the dog. I knew the moment Caesar let go he would start barking again, and wake up the whole household. I went up to Monsieur Valleray, whom I recognized, and I said to him, 'Take my hand and appear to be very friendly with me.' Monsieur Valleray understood at once, and seized my hand. I then spoke very sweetly to him and began to caress him like that, at the same time saying to Caesar, 'This is my good friend, Monsieur Valleray. We love him very much and you must not hurt him or bark at him. Don't be angry, you see he is one of our friends.' In fact, I behaved very affectionately to Monsieur Valleray and this made a great impression on Caesar and he finally let go his hold. I then went and got the key of the garden gate, and I led Monsieur Valleray out of it, holding his hand as if I were in love with him, because this terrible Caesar looked very suspicious and I did not dare to trust him. Then I went back to the house, trembling all over lest all this noise had awakened dear mamma."

This explanation, of course, completely restored the young girl's reputation, and then the only things to be cleared up were the reason for Valleray's being in the garden at that hour and the identity of the person who closed the window in the hôtel de France. Both these mysteries were cleared up when Lady Tartuffe broke down and admitted that Valleray had jumped out of the window after visiting her.

It is easy to see that the rôle of Lady Tartuffe offered no such dramatic possibilities as those to which the great tragédienne had been accustomed. Nothing but her personal relations with Delphine could have induced her to take the part at all. The fact was, Rachel was under a heavy obligation to Delphine even when at the height of her fame. As the daughter of a Jewish peddler it was not easy for her to storm the portals of the boulevard Saint-Germain. No one could do this for her so well as Delphine, whose social position, coupled with her artistic contacts, made her an ideal mediator. Rachel's lack of education was of course an impediment, which indeed she frankly admitted. To a member of the Académie who so admired her diction on the stage that he told her she had saved the French language from destruction she replied, "Yes, sir, and I deserve all the more credit as I can hardly speak it correctly."

Very likely Rachel would not have stooped to comedy while her reputation as a tragédienne was at its height, but in the six years that elapsed between her performance of Cléopâtre and the production of Lady Tartuffe things had happened to the great tragédienne. Comte Walewski, who had set her up in a palatial mansion in Paris, had now withdrawn his protection, and she had begun to have a premonition of the pulmonary affection which four years later was to carry her to the grave. Though tremendous throngs still crowded the theater whenever her name appeared upon the bills, people were whispering that Ristori, the great Italian actress, would soon drive her off the stage. The director of the Comédie-Française was growing restive under her exactions, and she had an altercation with him which resulted in her refusing for a time to renew her contract. Delphine at once came to the rescue and planned to build a theater in the garden back of her house in the rue de Chaillot where Rachel was to act. This generous project came to naught, as the manager of the Comédie-Française patched up his difference with her. But the incident was an added evidence of Delphine's loyalty and may have been the cause of Rachel's willingness to play the part of Lady Tartuffe.

It is hard to believe that Delphine's devotion to the great actress was based on personal affection. These two women had no common background. Their modes of living were as far apart as the poles. What drew Delphine to Rachel was wholly appreciation of the value of artistic accomplishment. You cannot read a line of the Lettres parisiennes without being conscious of the writer's artistic temperament. In recounting the incidents of her daily life you can see that her thoughts were always centered on what was beautiful rather than on what was useful. Paris, she says, is equipped with every sort of convenience, but it is spoiled by being so habitable. On purely aesthetic grounds she hated to see the passing of the old régime. When princesse Hélène who had married the exiled duc d'Orléans visited Paris, Delphine reminded her that she would find none of the poetry amidst which she had been brought up in Germany. "The reign of the tricolor is the reign of prose. We have no princesses. We have no poets. At our court the great ladies have no more honor than the humblest peasant." And in another passage she exclaims, "I bemoan the king of ancient France, the chivalric, brilliant, and poetic France; and I vainly seek in the bourgeois France of to-day that flower of courtesy, that perfume of royalty, that majestic benevolence which is gone forever." Such expressions appear a bit extravagant when we turn our thoughts upon the millions of humble citizens whom that majestic benevolence never reached. Looking at it as a whole the nation could view with equanimity the decline of royal power. Still, Delphine was quite right in asserting that by gaining individual liberty the people were throwing away many of the things that lent embellishment to life.

It was ridiculous, she thought, to talk so much about equality. As an ideal, it was perfect. But it was not a fact. A sluggard is not the equal of a man who works. Nature never intended that all men should be equal. Some are endowed with force, others with intelligence, others with beauty. All that society can do is to offer compensations to those who are not blessed by nature. You can give riches to those who lack force, education to those who lack intelligence, position to those who have no beauty. Society can pass laws to give consolation to the unfortunate, but it is beyond the power of law to make the fool and wise man equal.

Taken as a whole, the period in which she lived was a period of great material prosperity. France was extending her commerce all over the world, and was adding much to her colonial possessions. Algeria was conquered and made

a part of France. The Marquesas Islands were wrested from
the United States. Cochinchina was being opened up to lucrative trade. Constantinople was captured, and many of the
seaports along the eastern end of the Mediterranean fell
under French control. In 1837 the first railroad in France
was built, extending from Paris to Saint-Germain. In 1839
Daguerre introduced his invention of making photographs on
a sensitized plate. Gas was being installed on the boulevards
which had hitherto been equipped with nothing but oil lamps.
Business was advancing with rapid strides. Everybody
seemed to be making money. The streets of Paris were so
filled with bustling crowds that one could hardly make his
way about; and they were so infested with robbers that it
was not safe to go out at night. As Delphine said, "France
has become a nation of wig-makers, and everything that isn't
useful has been abolished." She remarked that people did not
seem to realize that the things which have no utility are the
only things that make a nation great. They have come to place
a money value on everything, and do not see that the real
things of life, the things which give durable satisfaction, cannot be bought with money. She hated to see people with no
taste crowding into everything; and she commented on the
grotesquely dressed women who drove up to the Louvre every
day in their pretentious equipages. When Paris was being
fortified in 1840, she felt it was turning the city into an armed
camp and bringing the intellectual pre-eminence of Paris
to an end.

According to her it was the heyday of tradespeople. In

their hands were concentrated all the money as well as all the power. The sugar-coated bourgeoisie, as she loved to call them, were making France the laughing-stock of Europe. Always lavishly attired, but in execrable taste, they had no ideas of their own, but were always looking around to see how others behaved. "Finding themselves by a stroke of luck in a sphere with which they were unacquainted, they have improvised a code of elegance which will soon become generally adopted if ladies of refinement don't use their influence to combat it." She saw in their antics an utter absence of individual initiative. "There are no longer any genuine women. Their place has been taken by an aggregation of mechanical dolls."

During all the years while she was contributing to La Presse the throne was occupied by Louis-Philippe, the "citizen king." Though of royal lineage he had divested himself of all his titles, and before coming to the throne had led the life of an ordinary citizen. As a school-teacher in Switzerland and as a traveller in the United States he had become thoroughly imbued with democratic principles and had held himself out as a firm advocate of the doctrine of equal rights. The royal authority came to him not by usurpation but by election of the chambre des députés. Instead of being called the king of France he was given the title "King of the French." It was understood that he held office merely as a representative of the people. And he agreed to rule according to the terms of a charter which made him subservient in all respects to the deputies elected by the people. His authority was so limited that neither he nor his subjects knew whether France should be designated as a kingdom or republic.

The scheme of government had been framed by men who honestly believed they were establishing a republic, but very soon after the scheme was adopted they saw that what they had set in motion was in no sense a government by the people, since the property qualification of electors was so high that only an infinitesimal number of the people had a right to vote. The franchise was restricted to those who paid in taxes two hundred francs a year, which meant that in a population of thirty-four million only two hundred and forty thousand had a voice in the election of deputies; and moreover there were one hundred and fifty public functionaries who had a right to sit in the chambre by virtue of their office. As time wore on, the complaint was often heard that the deputies kept themselves in power by distributing these offices among their friends and were much more interested in buying votes than in attending to the country's business. Some of them became so obsessed with their own importance that they paid no deference to the king. A story went the rounds that on one occasion the king met a deputy on the street and stood with head uncovered till the deputy told him to put on his hat.

Delphine, regretting as she did the passing of the old régime, was shocked at the indignities that were heaped upon the king. "It is not his fault," she wrote, "that this epoch is not more beautiful, that stucco has taken the place of solid mouldings, that papier-mâché has replaced bronze, that we have bald deputies instead of ambassadors with long perukes, that frock coats are worn in place of velvet uniforms, and black cravats in place of lace jabots." She did not think the thing would last. She felt that if France were to have a king at all he must be given real power. Louis-Philippe, she said, had only the semblance of power. He could declare war, but he could not carry it on because the people had control of the purse strings. In her Lettres parisiennes, Delphine grew more and more insistent that a new form of government must be brought about. She denounced Thiers, who, she said, had great talent but was obsessed by the idea that he was a great statesman. She asserted that France was governed by the rich electors and that Thiers by pretending to be a great statesman had become the laughing-stock of Europe.

This plain language did much to add to the unrest, particularly as it echoed the sentiments of Delphine's husband, whose paper had now become the main vehicle for disseminating the popular antagonism to the government. Feeling was growing so bitter that many were talking of insurrection. This catastrophe the king tried to avert by changing his ministers, but he was so vacillating that, as Delphine declares, he reminded one of a farmer who let the summer slip by while he was deciding which horse to hitch to the plow. After a while the situation became so menacing that the deputies virtually selected the ministry themselves. By forming coalitions of members holding divergent principles they sought to stay the clamor of the people, but in the nature of things such coalitions could not expect long life. According to Delphine, the life of a ministry was little more than a day. It was becoming monotonous, she said, to see men going out of office one day and coming back the next.

In 1847 her friend Lamartine published his Histoire des girondins which openly advocated a republic; and the smouldering disaffection burst into flames. In February, 1848, insurrection broke out in Paris. La Presse demanded the abdication of the king, and Delphine's husband became the foremost champion of those who favored a republic. Hoping to appease the people, Louis-Philippe, on February 24th, abdicated in favor of his son. Many of the deputies refused to assent to this change, and the turmoil increased still further. Girardin, expecting daily to be arrested, shut himself up in his office and communicated with his wife only by letter. One day the insurgents fired on the sentinel posted near her house. She wrote to her husband and asked if she should hide their valuables so as to save them if the house were pillaged. "No," he wrote back, "I have nothing to save or hide. If the guard is overpowered and rioters try to enter our house, open the door wide and be exceedingly polite. That is the best form of resistance." She followed his instructions to the letter. Whenever she went out the servants were told to say to anyone who tried to break in, "Monsieur and madame de Girardin will not permit their fellow citizens to steal. We offer you as a present anything in our house which you desire."

On June 25th, Girardin was arrested, and wrote to her from his cell asking her to send him some fresh linen and a cloak to lie down on. She complied with his request but heard nothing further from him for five days. Then she got a letter saying he was well and comfortable, and soon after he was released.

That was the end of the Lettres parisiennes. The election of Louis-Napoléon as the president of the new republic, followed by the coup d'état in which he established the Second Empire, swept away many of the incongruities which she had been assailing; and the few remaining years of her life were given up to the amenities of society and the production of a few light pieces of writing for the stage.

Among the literary men who basked occasionally in the sunshine of Delphine's genial society was the whimsical Honoré de Balzac whose infatuation dated back to the days when everyone had been captivated by her youth and beauty. Nature certainly never designed Balzac to be a successful aspirant for the female heart. He was short and fat and awkward. His manners were crude and his taste was execrable. Though he possessed a marvellous capacity to depict the character of all sorts of people, his own personality and the impression that it had on others were entirely outside his power to comprehend. His personal vanity was so excessive that it was constantly leading him into actions in which he was utterly grotesque. Ten years of unremitting industry in the writing of novels had brought him no pecuniary reward, but nothing could shake his confidence in his literary skill. When he became acquainted with Delphine he was being chased by creditors and only a few of his intimates were kept informed of his address. Apparently she was one of the first to recognize his talent. At any rate she took compassion on him and sought to admit him into the circle of her friends.

That was rather an uphill task. He never fitted into the literary set that frequented her salon. Most of her friends thought him a boor and laughed at his grotesque efforts to make himself conspicuous. Her nature was too kindly to take offense because he put on airs, and in one of his letters we find him calling her his pupil—without any justification so far as one can see. He seems to have imposed a little on her good nature and one day she permitted him to take her out to drive in his tilbury. In the course of the drive he overturned the tilbury and she came back with a lacerated hand. He was then addressing her as "divine Delphine" and was asking her to write the preface to his Études des femmes. He labored under the delusion that he had touched her heart. The truth was, he was writing stories for her husband's newspaper and Delphine deemed it prudent to humor him so far as she could without overstepping the bounds of propriety.

There came a time when nothing but Delphine's intercession kept the writer and the publisher from blows. Balzac, after ten years of unrewarded application, had emerged from obscurity and had reached a level in the world of literature which he believed entitled him to an increase in his pecuniary reward. Émile de Girardin, to whose publications Balzac was still in the habit of contributing, was a little tardy in recognizing Balzac's worth, and an altercation arose between them in which each used language which the other vehemently resented. The quarrel coming to Delphine's ears, she sought out Balzac and attempted to appease his wrath. Two weeks later she wrote to him a conciliatory letter pointing out the wisdom of patching up their differences and saying that neither he nor her husband was showing common sense. She closed by inviting him to dinner, and declared that her sister was particularly eager to meet him. Three months later she invited him again, and, both of these invitations being declined, she published an amusing little story entitled La canne de M. de Balzac, in which she endeavored to flatter his vanity. This little story had the desired effect, and Balzac and her husband laid aside the gloves.

Twice in her Lettres parisiennes she says a word in praise of Balzac. In one of his novels he had claimed that a woman's real love does not begin until she is mature. "M. de Balzac," she comments, "is bound to portray passion where he finds it, and he certainly can no longer find it in the girl of sixteen. . . . The dreams of youth to-day are dreams of ambition. No young girl marries to-day except to gain position. . . . Look at any of the women who now shine in society. They all began with an ambitious marriage. They all looked forward to being rich, to being countesses, marchionesses, or duchesses. It is only after they have learned the folly of these vanities that their hearts have turned to love. When they are twenty-eight or thirty they fall desperately in love with the young man whom they refused at seventeen."

Four years later Delphine again took up her pen in defense of Balzac. The critics were denouncing him for putting on the stage a play which depicted thievery and assassination. "It is not," she says, "the fault of modern writers that their descriptions of life contain no poetry. The cleverest architect can build only with the materials which he has at hand. . . . In olden days the most commonplace things were idealized, language was pompous, images were fantastic. People talked in the language of the gods. Nowadays, on the contrary, the most beautiful ideals are presented in vulgar dress."

No better illustration can be given of Delphine's feeling for Balzac. She recognized him as an accurate delineator of the times. But between them there was no real bond of friendship. She was a poet; he was a realist. So long as he lived she continued to invite him to her house, and sometimes he refused on the ground that she was surrounded by all the literary lions while he was only a compositor of prose. This confession did not come from him, however, until he was drawing to the end. His eyes had become opened to the absurdity of imagining that he and Delphine stood on common ground.

Of all the literary geniuses who fell under the spell of Delphine's personality there was none more steadfast in his admiration than the illustrious poet and romanticist, Victor Hugo. When he was a rising young poet he had joined enthusiastically in the eulogies with which Delphine was being welcomed into the coterie of literary people, and she on her part was one of the first to recognize Hugo's marvellous imaginative power. She was but two years his junior, and it is manifest from his earliest letters that he was fascinated by her. His estimation of Delphine's artistic capacity was unquestionably warped. But the rapture which overwhelmed him when he first gazed into her beautiful eyes never faded away, and to the end of her life he never wavered from his early conception of her as one of the most brilliant writers of the day. In all his letters to her there was an air of gallantry that is eloquent of the promptings of his heart. The first letter that we have was written to accept an invitation to hear one of his brother authors read at her house. "With great pleasure," he writes, "I will hear him read at your house and in your presence. Permit me, madame, to lay at your feet my most sincere homage." Rather stately language, one might think; but this was always a characteristic habit of Hugo's.

A little later, in securing theater tickets for Delphine, he writes, "Excuse this scrawl. My eyes are worse than ever. May your lovely eyes have pity on mine, which are neither lovely nor good. I throw myself at your feet." And again, "You were very charming, madame, and very generous to me day before yesterday. I was overwhelmed and confused, when I left you, for leaving you so late." She had now, for the present at any rate, abandoned poetry and was immersed in her Lettres parisiennes. But this made no breach in their cordial relations. "I intended yesterday to bring my answer to you in person as soon as I had read your enchanting Courrier. Something kept me at my house, but I have no complaint as it brought me two letters from you instead of one. I am going to dine with you to-morrow, and then will you permit me to kiss your beautiful hands and offer you the homage of my most tender respect." He signs this letter "Victor."

On Hugo's election to the Académie française in 1841, Delphine seized the opportunity to laud his merits. He won by only two votes, and she did not shrink from telling the public whence the opposition came. It was from the trades-folk, who were either too busy or too ignorant to familiarize themselves with Hugo's marvellous intellectual achievements. Those who think and feel, those who are famous in the world of letters, were unanimous in favoring his election. "The Académie needs a few great geniuses like Hugo to prevent its stately members from falling into a doze."

Then followed a period of ten years in which a profound change was coming about in the intellectual activity of Hugo. Like Delphine he was abandoning poetry and allowing his thoughts to dwell on politics. More and more he was absorb-ing the revolutionary ideas that were set forth in the news-paper published by Delphine's husband. When the republic was proclaimed in 1848 he took his seat in the assemblée constituante where he remained till Louis-Napoléon overthrew the republic and declared himself emperor. Hugo was forced to flee, and remained in exile for nineteen years, thus termi-nating his intimate relations with Delphine.

Still, in the solitude of his home in Jersey where he had taken refuge, he pined for the companionship of Delphine. He begged her to come to him and read the drama which she was now writing for the stage. She shared his indignation at the coup d'état which had placed a Napoleon once more upon the throne. "We all love you," he writes. "When I think of France (and I am always thinking of her) I think of you."

Once, she braved the hostility of Napoleon and made the journey. After she had returned to Paris he wrote her about her latest poem, which she had left for him to read. "You have composed a somber and charming poem," he declared. "The strange and passing fancy of a heart torn in opposite directions by a double love you have painted admirably. In your book there is a charm of mystery, a pathos, and a grace, which you alone possess."

A few months later, to enliven his exile, she sent him a copy of her Lettres parisiennes which had just been published in book form, and he acknowledged the gift thus: "Just now one of my friends was sitting at one side of the fireplace and I at the other when the vicomte de Launay came and sat down between us. In plain language, we talked of only you. Exiles generally can weep or laugh, but you triumphed over everything, for we thought of nothing but your bewitching smile. Thanks to you, despite the snow and the misery of our exile, we had for a moment at Marine-Terrace a real salon of which you were the queen and we your subjects. What a charming book you have sent me. Once I used to read its separate sheets as they came out from the press; now I read it page by page. I find there ancient diamonds and new pearls —and, scattered among them, all sorts of exquisite things. You say, 'All is lost, the women are on the side of the victors and against the vanquished.' I say, 'All is saved, for a woman is with us, and what a woman! It is you.' Yes, you are a real woman, for you have beauty and a tender heart—you understand. You smile, you love. You are a real woman with a power to teach both sexes. You know how to tell men where to fix their aspirations and to tell women where to place their affections."

After her death, while his heart was still tingling with emotion, he jotted down some verses which show how deep his feelings for her were:

"Jadis je vous disais: Vivez, régnez, madame!
Le salon vous attend, le succès vous réclame!
Le bal éblouissant pâlit quand vous partez!
Soyez illustre et belle! Aimez! riez! chantez!
Vous avez la splendeur des astres et des roses!
Votre regard charmant, où je lis tant de choses,
Commente vos discours légers et gracieux.
Ce que dit votre bouche étincelle en vos yeux."

MARIE d'AGOULT

MARIE D'AGOULT, a contemporary of Delphine Gay, is known chiefly by her effort to arouse the public to a more liberal attitude regarding women's rights. That was a movement which made much headway in the earlier half of the nineteenth century, though its progress was not easily discernible in the realm of government or finance. To the present day, women do not sit in the chambre des députés or hold property entirely free from marital control. What they have gained is greater freedom to regulate their private lives. For that they are indebted in no small measure to Marie d'Agoult.

*

TO SAY that Marie d'Agoult was one of the leaders in the movement for the enfranchisement of women would be to accord her a position which she hardly claimed. It is true she published a couple of essays in which she cried out against the wrong inflicted on women in withholding from them all participation in governmental affairs. But she took no part in organized effort to modify the laws, and her influence as a reformer lay almost wholly in the boldness with which she established her own individuality in defiance of the recognized moral code. Her wealth and social standing

MARIE D' AGOULT

phere. Though the most exclusive society in France was always open to her, she never felt that it was quite her own. Born in Frankfort and reared by a protestant mother, her intellectual processes always ran in German channels, and her sentiments were more or less tinctured by ideas that were current in the land where she was born.

It did not take her long to find out that in the eyes of those about her she had a considerable matrimonial value. With an income of three hundred thousand francs, she was deemed a très-bon-parti, and in the five years that elapsed between her leaving the convent and her marriage there was a steady procession of suitors at her door. The main topics of conversation in her family were the titles and pecuniary standing of men who sought her hand. It seemed to her as if they talked of nothing but figures, and she was appalled to learn that marriage seemed to be little more than a pecuniary negotiation. Finally she became so sick of the whole business that she told her mother she didn't want to hear any more about it—she would leave it to her family advisers to pick out a husband for her and she would abide by their decision.

Clothed with this mandate they succeeded in arranging an alliance which was admirable from a material point of view. Le comte d'Agoult was related to many of the best families in France and was a nephew of the chief equerry of the dauphine. He was himself a colonel of cavalry in the service of the king. His means, though less than those of his bride, were ample, and he had acquired an enviable reputation for bravery and for devotion to his profession. Unfortunately, however, he was utterly indifferent to art, to music, to literature, and to all those things that add embellishment to life. Being twenty years older than Marie, his habits had become permanently fixed before he married her. The result was that he was never able to adjust himself to her tastes or to share in any of her aspirations. She wrote later, in her Mémoires, that in all her married life with him she never had a single hour of joy.

That was the situation when Liszt came into Marie's life. She was then twenty-eight, and the mother of two children. Franz was twenty-two. At the age of ten he had been recognized in his native town in Hungary as a prodigy. Two years later his parents brought him to Paris where he electrified the musical world by his marvellous genius as a pianist. Arrangements were made for him to give exhibitions of his skill at all the great houses. He was even taken to England, where he played before King George IV. As he grew up, his services as a teacher were in constant demand, and he accepted some of the offers that were made to him, though he relied chiefly on his concerts to provide him with a livelihood. Naturally, of course, his ambition was to become a great composer, and he composed at that time a number of sonatas which showed his extraordinary artistic power. But throughout this period his emotions were leading him into all sorts of vagaries. At one time he was about to throw aside his musical efforts and become a priest. Franz stopped short of holy orders, but his journey into the mystic doctrines of the Church gave him a new conception of his profession. He became convinced tha art had no value except as a means to glorified life. Art was nothing but the handmaid of religion. While it was through science that God taught men the material things of life, it was through art alone He showed them what was beautiful. The musician, therefore, was nothing but the minister of God, and the development of the emotions—including love—was inseparable from all that was divine. Liszt was in this state of exaltation when he ran across Chopin, the sensitive and delicate youth whose musical compositions were already startling the fashionable society of Paris.

We have now reached the year 1833. Franz and Chopin had become fast friends. Both were creatures of sentiment, living in the clouds, dreaming of things ethereal, of music, and of love. Franz had grown into manhood, tall, and spare, and erect. When his fingers wandered over the keys, his expression became so intense that he seemed to have lost all touch with the material things around him. He had the manner of one inspired by God. Chopin, less spectacular in appearance, shrank from public applause. One night, however, Franz determined to bring him out. He organized a surprise party. A dozen of the best-known musicians gathered at Chopin's quarters, each bringing his contribution of food and drink, and forced Chopin to take his seat at the piano. Among the auditors were several singers, a few composers, a poet, George Sand,—and Marie d'Agoult, who had been introduced by the composer Berlioz. Not long after, Franz agreed to come to the house of a marquise whom Marie knew and play the piano informally. Marie was invited to come and hear him. From the moment she laid eyes on him, it was like an apparition. His large sea-green eyes flashed like waves in the sunlight. He had a sad but overpowering expression, and a wandering, distracted air. He took his seat by her side and began to talk as if he had known her all his life. "Impetuously he filled my soul with ideas which were unlike anything I had heard from those with whom I was used to converse. . . . I went home late. I could scarcely sleep, and my mind was filled with strange dreams." The next day Marie invited him to her house. Her interest in music was the pretext. She found that he shared her views on politics and society, and they opened their hearts freely to each other.

Marie naïvely declares in her Mémoires that there was no coquetry or gallantry between them, but it requires no profound insight into human nature to see that she was completely carried off her feet. Her love of music, the boredom of her married life, the mystical character of the young virtuoso, contributed to make him the embodiment of her dreams. She saw in him not only a lover but a liberator. She had always been considered cold, and he was the first man who had awakened in her an ardent passion. Her husband was so much her senior that Liszt's youth merely added to his charms. Soon they were seeing each other almost every day.

When summer came, she went as usual to her place in the country, but she could not keep him out of her thoughts. After six weeks, which seemed to her a century, she wrote and invited him to visit her. She felt like a person who has long been starved. "My youth, without expansion, stifled midway in its development, had been only a prolonged childhood. My mind was no less eager to learn than my heart to love," and when he arrived "we both felt that we were on the verge of culpability." When he sat down at the piano, he created harmonies which opened heaven to her. After a few days each saw that an irresistible power was bringing them together. They began to give voice to their passion. The effect was instantaneous—"a sudden appeasement of the violences of youth, a calmness of the soul and of the senses such as always establishes itself between two passionate persons from the moment when each confesses to the other the secret of their mutual love."

Soon after, she lost one of her children, and that only made matters worse. She and her husband relapsed into silence and the distance between them grew wider. Liszt came to see her, but both felt that their liaison could not continue while she was plunged in grief. He fled from Paris and buried himself in the country. Six months later, feeling that he could endure the absence no longer, he returned to Paris and found her more wrapped up in him than ever. At their first interview he burst out, "We must go away." He seized her in his arms and cried out, "There is nothing in the world but love. I love you and I am going to break off your chains. In life and death we are joined together." In telling the story later, Marie says his vehemence was so terrific that all her power of resistance was gone. Eight days later she quitted France.

They had no definite plan except to go to Switzerland where they could live in solitude and where Liszt could compose. They went first to Lake Wallenstadt and then to Bex on the Rhone. When autumn came they moved to Geneva and put up at a modest hostelry which they used as their head-quarters while searching for a simple apartment. They had no difficulty in making a choice, for they were not exacting. All they wanted was a place big enough for Liszt's piano. For a few weeks they lived in ecstasy—Franz devoting most of his time to music and Marie reading and writing when she was not gazing into his big dreamy eyes.

One day she received a letter from her mother expressing no indignation and begging Marie to come back and live with her. To this request Marie sent back an unqualified re-fusal. The honeymoon had not yet reached its second quarter. As she declared later, "My passion for Franz had grown deeper in the solitude of the last few months. It had become a sort of fanaticism. I saw in him a being apart from all others, superior to anyone I had ever known. . . . I was in a state of mystic delirium, appointed by God to serve this divine genius who had nothing in common with other men and who was above all human laws."

This letter, however, gave occasion for the first jar in their relations. When she had read it Franz asked in an off-hand manner if it contained any news from France. She was shocked by his lack of comprehension. He seemed to be thinking only of extraneous matters, and to attach no im-portance to the stupendous sacrifice she had made in giving herself up to him.

The next shock came when Franz ran across a youngster

whose musical talent aroused his interest, and he asked Marie
to let the boy come and share their apartment. It pained her
dreadfully to realize that Franz should be willing to allow an
outsider to enter into their lives. How, she thought, could
Franz fail to see that she had given up her home, her husband, her fortune, everything, for him? He was asking her
to take up one of his protégés and put him in the place of
her own children whom she had abandoned. It caused her a
pang to feel for the first time that he could care for anything
in which they did not have a common interest.

It was too late, however, to indulge in recriminations. She
had broken with the past and it would not do now to quarrel
with Franz. Their first child was coming in December and
she felt more and more dependent on the marvellous genius
with whom she had thrown in her lot. There was no diminution
of her love, but it was becoming gradually less impetuous;
and she could not afford to be insistent that he give up his
whole life to her.

The truth is, Franz was more and more inclined to break
away from the monotony of Marie's unceasing devotion.
Busybodies were already talking about this Juno and the
tall, loose-jointed youth with disheveled hair and delicate,
almost feminine, features. Geneva was full of fugitive lovers,
but this pair showed by their dignified bearing and intellectual
appearance that they were not of the ordinary kind. In fact,
Liszt was too great a celebrity to keep his identity long con-
cealed. To Marie's chagrin, before long the story of their
escapade was in everybody's mouth. People were whispering

that she was an adventuress who had got the great virtuoso under her spell.

What made it worse was that they were now no longer allowed to live their lives alone. A Russian lady of social position and with much musical talent arranged to have Franz give her lessons, and she took great pains to introduce him into Geneva society. He became, of course, a public favorite and before the winter was over he was persuaded to give a concert. He even went so far as to insist that Marie occupy a box. She was shocked to realize that he had so little solicitude for her feelings. It almost seemed as if he wished to advertise her humiliating position. She complied with his wishes, but the episode left a deep wound in her heart.

It was while Marie was in Switzerland that she first became really intimate with George Sand. The first meeting between them had occurred a few years before, when they met casually at the theater. They met again at the Chopin party but apparently had no opportunity to become acquainted. In the spring of 1835, after Liszt had come into the picture, Sand, who was always keyed up by amorous adventures, wrote to Marie, "Beautiful, fair-haired countess, I do not know you personally, but I have heard Franz talk about you. . . . I cherish a constant hope of being allowed to go and see you. . . . I hear that you want to become a writer. . . . Do so whilst you still have genius, whilst a divinity dictates to you and you do not merely write from memory." Marie was delighted at the thought of knowing the author of the daring novels that everybody was discussing, and Sand was burning to be ad-

mitted into the aristocratic circles from which she had hitherto
been excluded. But what brought them closer than all else was
the similarity of their emotion. Sand had just returned from
her escapade with Alfred de Musset, and Marie was about to
start on hers with Liszt. They came together and laid bare
their souls. Liszt, who had long been intimate with Sand, was
filled with joy on seeing them become close friends. Just before the flight he invited the two women to dine with him at
his mother's house, and Sand was admitted into the secret of
their plans. Needless to say, she was enthusiastic over the
project, and promised to visit them in Switzerland.

One of the first letters that Marie wrote after she got settled
was to Sand. "I am burning to dispute the literary palm,"
she wrote, and a spirited literary correspondence followed.
In January, 1836, their intimacy had proceeded so far that
Sand dedicated her Simon to the "patricienne." The correspondence was interrupted in the following spring by Sand's
legal difficulties in getting a divorce from her husband, but
when that was accomplished she went to Switzerland and
spent a few weeks with Marie.

It was now becoming clear that Geneva could not hold
them longer. Both Marie and Franz were chafing under the
pettiness of their lives. Marie's love had developed into a sort
of worship and she felt that Liszt must be given a wider opportunity to display his marvellous talent. Franz suggested
that they go to Italy and she was overjoyed at the thought of
visiting the land of poetry and song. Their sojourn in Geneva,
which had opened with a complete consecration of themselves

to each other, had ended, if not with disappointment, at least with a saner understanding of the difference in their mental and moral make-up. They had come to know each other's impelling forces. Commenting, later, upon this period, Marie wrote, "It was a period of devouring passion, a cruel conflict between our two natures, both sincere, noble, and devoted, but proud, unsatisfied—he feeling and demanding love as a young man, unquenchable, of vigorous vitality, and I a woman defying destiny, broken down by grief, a dreamer, turning my face against reality to lose myself in an impossible idealism."

They did not go at once to Italy, but to Paris, where Franz wanted to give a few concerts to keep the pot boiling. It was a dreadful ordeal for Marie. Her old family friends refused to see her, and the children whom she had had by her husband were not permitted to share her company. So she and Liszt hired an apartment in a modest hotel and wrote to Sand urging her to take a room in the same hotel. She came, and stayed through the winter. The place was overrun with Sand's friends of the artistic set—a set to which Marie now aspired to belong. Sand was just beginning her liaison with Liszt's friend Chopin, but Marie was not familiar enough with artists' habits to realize what was going on. Sand's oddities were amusing and gave an added piquancy to her charm.

In January, 1837, Sand went back to her country place at Nohant after securing from Marie a promise that she would visit her there. In February Marie went to Nohant and was followed three weeks later by Franz. With a short interruption this visit lasted three months, and it gave Marie a good opportunity to study the strange character of Sand. "Poor, great woman," is her characterization. "The sacred flame that God has placed in her finds nothing to devour outside and so consumes in her all that remains of faith, youth, hope." This comment seems to describe Marie better than Sand, for in another passage Marie says, "George is the only woman with whom I could live long without fatigue." But her eyes were being opened to the gulf that separated them. "My stay at Nohant has given solidity to our friendship. I know better now how to judge her good and bad traits." Again she says, "George is an incorrigible child. She is a weak woman even in her audacity, changeable in her sentiments and opinions, illogical, her life guided by chance, not by reason or experience."

Whatever effect the visit may have had on Marie's relations with Sand, it gave her an opportunity to get some hold on herself. "Though George's nature is not in harmony with mine, she has cheered me up. From an extreme distrustfulness of myself, I have come to have a just appreciation of my value." She was already coming to see that she had been chasing a chimera, and undoubtedly Sand's worldly wisdom did much to open Marie's eyes. She was still infatuated, but she had at least come to know that it was infatuation and not an affection based on any rational grounds. That was a step forward, because, though it did not shake her determination to cling to Franz, it led her to reflect upon her own capacity to do things for herself. Whereas Franz was all a creature of impulse, she liked to analyze every emotion so as to make a record of her individuality. The idea of writing her Mémoires had already taken shape, and she was beginning to realize that she would some day have to face the ending of her liaison with Liszt.

Some of the entries in her journal show that she felt no remorse about her escapade. "I have always seen lovers, even those whose love grew and was sanctified by time, regret the first hours of budding affection and describe them as a period of illusion. Is it not childish to bemoan the errors without which love perhaps would never have been born?" Even after she had become conscious that there must be divergent currents in their lives her adoration continued without a break. "People think him ambitious. He is not, for he knows the limits of things, and his perception of the infinite carries his soul far beyond all thought of glory and beyond all terrestrial joy. . . . It is with a love full of respect and sadness that I contemplate his beauty. . . . Often his gentle, veiled look is fixed on me with an indescribable expression of love and tenderness, which gives me a sense of happiness unknown to those who have not had such love."

Occasionally there is a note of helplessness without him. She had burned her bridges behind her, and could not easily contemplate the thought of giving him up. Her dependence on him was real though she always endeavored to give it a spiritual significance, as she did when she jotted down the confession, "In traversing new scenes with him I feel that he is my only support, and that I have no temple or country but in his heart."

Leaving Nohant in May they journeyed leisurely to Italy. In Lyon, where Franz had arranged to give a concert, they ran across the poet Louis de Ronchaud whom Marie describes as "the most devoted and tender of our friends," and at Saint-Point they stayed a few days with Lamartine. He entertained them royally in his sumptuous château and listened rapturously to Liszt's playing. He was so impressed by Marie's beauty that he wrote a poem under the inspiration of their visit.

They reached Lake Como in September and rented a villa at Bellaggio where they stayed three months. It was a second honeymoon. They spent their days basking in the sun and their evenings holding each other's hands. Her journal of those days is saturated and bubbling over with happiness. "Evening has arrived. The dark outlines of the mountains around us form a barrier which seems to forbid our thoughts going any further. Why, in fact, should we seek to go beyond? What is there in the world but work, and contemplation, and love?" "Festoons of amorous vines twine around each other this evening and their purple grapes hang lightly over our balcony."

One day they went to a fête in a neighboring village where she saw young girls bringing their baskets of fruit to the altar to receive a blessing, and her thoughts went back to the ancient sacrifices with their offerings to Venus.

Franz's twenty-sixth birthday occurred while they were at
Bellaggio. They celebrated it by a donkey-ride up the mountain, and in the evening fished by torchlight. "Sometimes I
am astonished to see him so gay and happy in the solitude
that is about us. . . . He, whose spirit is so communicative,
whose occupations have always been in the midst of things,
an artist, that is to say a man of sympathy, of emotion, of
fancy, now compresses all his faculties into the narrow frame
of a tête-à-tête. A poor piano, a few books, the conversation
of a serious woman, are all he asks."

In the ecstasy of her emotion, she sees in Italian art the
counterpart of her joy. Christianity had done all it could to
stifle art. "A religion which proscribes love as a shameful
weakness, how can it help art, which sees divinity in all material things and by so doing enlarges men's hearts? Polythe-
ism, which exalted and saw divinity in the passions, that is
to say in life, was it not more in sympathy with art than is
Christianity with its perpetual summons to an unknown mysterious life where there are no material things? . . . It was
not in sackcloth and ashes that the artists of the Renaissance
found their inspiration. It was in the arms of his young
mistresses, it was in the ecstasy of love, that Raphael dreamt
of the madonnas before whom all the world kneels in admiration. It was in the festivities of a sumptuous court that Leo-
nardo, the favorite of princes, conceived the plan of the Last
Supper."

Liszt responded to her cogitations, and compared love to
the flowers, which wilt under the piercing rays of the sun.

"Love is so strong that it crushes the heart. Under the inspiration of love the heart withers up and becomes a divine emotion. The moon gets its light from the sun, and gives a poetic, mysterious color to everything; but art gets its light only from the divine effulgence of love."

Marie did not let herself be carried into fantasies quite so deep as that, but, no less than Franz, she stood firm for the holiness of love. "When two rivers come together, amazed to find their current is no longer smooth, they quarrel and stir up mud and gravel from their beds. Then, fatigued by useless strife, they patch up their quarrels and flow peacefully to the sea. So two human beings, when they seek to unite their destinies, become ashamed of the resistance which their passions, their faults, and their virtues had at first caused them to offer. Our wrong inclinations have become exposed, for our sufferings have been given voice, and our complaints have so added to our sufferings that at last the deep love that brought us together outweighs all other considerations, and our two lives, indissolubly united, flow on in peace as if reflected from heaven."

Here, on the twenty-fifth of December, Marie gave her lover another child. They called it Cosima in memory of the happy days they had passed at Lake Como. As soon after as Marie was able to go about again they left the sunny slopes of Bellaggio and took up their abode in Milan. It was with deep forebodings that Marie saw her honeymoon reach its end. Much as she gloried in her lover's genius she knew she could not hold him when the applause of admiring multitudes was ringing in his ears. Her only hope was that the two children whom she had borne him would prevent his straying far. For a time her hope was fulfilled. The concerts which he gave in Milan were always before crowded houses, and the leaders of society showered him with attentions; but both he and Marie found those with whom they associated unable to appreciate the highest forms of musical composition. It was a relief to them, when the winter was over, to escape to Venice.

In Venice occurred a series of events which led inevitably to the final break. She has left us a brief memoir of the episode. One day Franz came to her with a newspaper telling of an inundation of the Danube which was causing misery to the people along its banks. His sympathy for his fellow-countrymen was so aroused that he told her he was going to Vienna to give a concert and turn the proceeds over to the suffering people. "It will take only eight days," he said; "What do you think?" She replied, "It is a noble thought"; but to herself she said, "Others could succor the poor, but who will aid me, alone and sick?" He started the next day, leaving her in Venice in the care of a young count whom he knew. The eight days slipped by and Franz did not return, but he sent newspapers which told of the marvellous success he was having. In her journal she writes, "It was beyond anything ever before heard of in Vienna. He was the equal of Mozart and Beethoven. Crowned heads asked to hear him in their family circles. A rain of gold and flowers fell at his feet, and at the end of his first concert the audience carried him off in triumph, great noblemen joining in the procession. Magnificent presents were piled up on his table. He received most flattering offers to write an opera, to direct concerts." Then came letters from him, short, and, as it seemed to Marie, cold. He wrote as if it were nothing, mentioning names of great people as if that did not amount to anything, but there was a false ring in all he wrote, entirely out of harmony with all he had been boasting to Marie about his disdain of the world and his determination to live in seclusion with her. Fifteen days passed and his letters said nothing about returning. His letters became more infrequent and names of various ladies appeared in them. One was on paper with a lady's seal on it, and it seemed to Marie to be dictated by a woman.

Marie was so upset that she fell ill and had to go to bed. The friend in whose care she had been placed wrote to Franz begging him to come back at once. This brought an answer urging Marie to go to Vienna. She fainted and for several days lay between life and death. When she recovered she wrote to Franz, "You ask me to join you. It is six hundred miles to Vienna and I can scarcely walk from my bed to my chair. You say you cannot come to me. You leave to another the care of my poor life. If I died you would have to come, or would you leave to others the duty of closing my eyes and placing a stone on my grave? Franz, Franz, is it you who has thus abandoned me?"

That letter brought him back. She fell into his arms with the words: "Pray God I may love you as I have done in the past." But she saw that his whole attitude had changed. He told her that he had made a great deal of money and had given it to the poor. In two years, he said, he could lay up a fortune, and he needed to do so for their daughter Blandine. Marie must now go back to Paris, reinstate herself with her family and re-establish her position. Marie found him hard, dry, ironic. He even asked her to accept as a lover the young man who had been looking after her. She said to him, "Let us try again."

So they patched things up, and resolved to try again. He went to Genoa and rented a magnificent villa, beautifully equipped, and for a while they lived there, but it was not at all to her taste. They did not stay there long. In August they were in Lugano, then in Milan, Bologna, Florence, and finally in Rome where they remained till the summer of 1839. There Marie gave birth to another child—a boy.

Franz was now wholly out of control. He was electrifying everyone by his marvellous gifts as a pianist, while Marie was at home caring for her three babies. Money from his concerts was pouring in so fast that he did not know what to do with it. The city of Bonn was raising a subscription for a statue of Beethoven. Bartolini who was to make the statue wrote to Liszt that the money was coming in too slowly, that the marble alone would cost one hundred and sixty thousand francs. Liszt wrote back that he would furnish the entire sum. He told Marie that he had made engagements to play all over Germany and that she could not keep up with his life. She must develop her own talents. "My talent," she replied, "is my love, my desire to please you."

He admitted that he had been unfaithful to her, and said he should probably be so again. A man is always liable to break his head against a wall, but he should be on his guard in future.

On the margin of this record we find in his handwriting these words: "You have a good memory for things that I have said, but perhaps you don't remember so well what you have said at various times. For my part, I have not forgotten, though I have tried to do so. When you reflect upon it you will find many things explained which now seem to you inexplicable because of the misunderstanding which has always existed between us."

The fact was, they had now reached the stage in their romantic adventure when each was holding himself or herself in reserve. They were playing the game of love, but their hearts were not wholly in the game. He was restless and wanted to get away. He felt that she was tying him down and preventing him from gaining the applause to which his genius entitled him. She realized that there was reason for his so feeling, and it made her miserable.

"It sometimes seems to me as if I did not know how to live. Ten years of suffering, of passion, of contact with the world, must have meant something to me, and now here I am with my first wrinkles, and white hair covering my temples."

She received a letter when he was away for a few days' visit. "A letter from him from Padua. His handwriting always causes me an inconceivable emotion, and his protestations of love come now as a surprise and fill my heart with rapture."

January 1st, 1839, at Florence. "Noon, sun. He has arrived. It seems as if I could not open my heart wide enough to take in all the joy that comes to me." Franz, too, felt his heart expand, and he jotted down these words: "I now have time to withdraw into myself, to think over the things that are in my heart, as Marie does. Like her I must listen long, long, to the voices that are in my heart, the echoes of her love."

Still, they were now talking of the separation that they both knew was at hand. "I have reproached him for his calmness in talking of our separation."

"Projects of Franz to consecrate four months of each year to his affairs, and live the rest of the time alone with me."

In Rome she writes, "I have never seen him so animated, so affectionate." And Franz said to her, "The three years I have passed with you have made a man of me."

Yet she could not shake off the feeling that she was ruining his life. "It was blind egotism that caused me to attach myself to him. . . . And he seems to be pained because he can give me so little joy."

In August, 1839, it had been agreed that she should go back to Paris and try to take up her old life again. In October, 1839, they parted. He accompanied her as far as Livorno, handed her a bouquet of flowers, and repeated the words he had said to her on July 30th, 1833, "You are not the woman that I need, but you are the one I want." She went to Paris to stay for a while with his mother, and he started for Vienna to begin his triumphal journey to all the capitals of Europe.

He was near but not quite at the end of his liaison with Marie. When he was in the midst of his triumphs in London, Marie went over to visit him. One of his friends who thought it was all over between them asked Franz about her and he replied, "If madame d'Agoult should ask me to throw myself out of that window, I should do so without a moment's hesitation."

That was heroic, but it does not sound like ardent love. In truth, the fire was almost extinct, and Franz was merely playing with the embers. Nothing but a flicker was left, but before it went out entirely Franz succeeded in fanning it once more into the semblance of a feeble flame. A ruined castle on an island in the Rhine appealed to his poetic fancy, and he leased it and wrote to Marie, "We have some years ahead of us yet. Did I say 'yet'? It seems to me the years ahead of us ought to be the only good, pure, tender, peaceful, indefinite years. If my doctrines are abominable, as you say, my dreams are sublime. . . . You were not deceived, Marie. We are not masters of each other. If we haven't acquired happiness, we may have acquired something better."

Marie waited not a moment to hurry to his new abode. She brought the children with her and they all lived there together through the summer. But it was no use. The great virtuoso had sources of inspiration other than the idyllic romanticism that she so persistently endeavored to weave about their lives. She returned to Paris, and he departed for Berlin to enter upon the period of his greatest professional success.

Not long after, she heard that he had attached himself to a famous dancer. She gritted her teeth, and jotted down in her journal these pathetic lines:

"No, you will not hear from her proud lips,
  In bidding you good-by, a reproof or a regret.
  There is no sting and no remorse for your light heart
        In this adieu.
  Perhaps you think that she, too, maddened by harsh rumor,
  Has forgotten the tears of yesterday and with fickle smile
  Has broken her plighted troth
        And passed along her way.
  You will never learn from her that she has not forgot,
  That on the solemn journey into eternal night
  Departing from her lover
        Her love remains."

She did not falsify when she declared that love remained. Her romance—the only one she ever had—was at an end, but the sentiment which gave it birth she carried to the grave. In 1845 she wrote in her journal, "I love him more deeply than I dare admit to myself." Again, "Eternity of love. People think I have ceased to love him. Some even think that my love has been succeeded by hatred. Profound error. The same ideal always." In later years, when she had made a place for herself in the world of literature, she looked back upon her days with Liszt as the momentous period of her life. "It is to him that I owe all," she said. "He inspired me with a great love. . . . I hope he will never feel regret or remorse for what he has made me suffer. Had he been what he should have been, I should have remained with him, and my name would never have emerged from obscurity." Certainly, so far as she was concerned, her escapade with Liszt caused no remorse. She recognized the necessity of its coming to an end because their natures did not permit them to pursue the same careers. He was an artist and could not have been expected to lead the prosaic life which her temperament required. But her romantic exaltation had been so deep, and, as she says, so pure, that nothing could ever make her regret what she had done.

After Liszt passed out of her life she felt as if her only prop was gone. Her mother had ceased communicating with her, and her husband apparently made no effort toward reconciliation. Her feelings were such that she could not ask to be forgiven, and she had no wish to renew relations with the frivolous society from which she had fled. Her associations with scholars in Geneva and in Italy had turned her mind toward serious studies. The taste for literature which she had acquired would have made the life of a society woman utterly distasteful to her. When in Geneva she had published, unsigned, a couple of short articles, one an essay on Victor Hugo, the other a translation of a book by Rousseau. Neither of these articles had attracted much attention, but they had given her some confidence in her ability to write. Now that all romance was banished from her life, she determined to devote the rest of her days to literary work.

One of the first persons whom she met after her return to Paris in 1839 was Delphine Gay. They met one evening after the opera. Delphine introduced herself and asked when she could call. She said she wanted Marie to meet Lamartine and Victor Hugo, and perhaps Théophile Gautier. A few days later Marie called on Delphine and met there Delphine's husband, Émile de Girardin, who impressed Marie as a keen observer, rather chary of conversation, though that caused little embarrassment, as his wife was an incessant talker. Not long after, Marie invited them to dinner, and Girardin seemed to take a great deal of interest in what she was planning to do. When he learned that she wanted to write, he offered to publish in La Presse anything that she cared to send him. She said she had been writing a critical article on some of Delaroche's paintings. He asked to see it and on looking it over remarked that it was excellent, but said that she must sign it. She told him she could not use a name which belonged to her husband as much as to herself. So they talked over a pseudonym and finally agreed upon Daniel Stern, the name under which thereafter all her writings were published. The article appeared in La Presse and created quite a stir. To criticize the most popular painter of the day was an audacious thing to do, but it caused a heated controversy which increased the circulation of La Presse and led to Marie's becoming the regular art critic for that journal.

From this modest beginning she was led to undertake more original work and in the next three years she published three novels, none of them of importance, but in one of them,

Nélida, published in 1846, she portrayed, in a way, the story of her relations with Liszt and gave expression to her belief in the right of women to follow the dictate of their hearts. She harbored no illusion about the superiority of man. The first revolution, she boasts, was in the Garden of Eden, and it was the work of a woman. The first man was content with the passive felicity that God had prepared for him, while the first woman obeyed the voice within her and cried out for liberty. "Risking all, she seized the forbidden fruit and led Adam to rebel."

Then, in 1847, Marie turned to more serious subjects and wrote her Essai sur la liberté. When she wrote this essay "her moral state," as one of her best friends said, "was that of a shipwrecked mariner thrown on a desert island, far from succor, with no resource beyond his own talent and labor. All that she had once possessed was gone except her liberty. The book was a portrayal of her heart long suppressed and afraid to expand, a heart that was measuring its own palpitations."

In the preface to this book she states that she felt the need of an outlet for her intellectual suffering, as Nélida had been the outlet for her heart's anguish. She attributes all her unhappiness to the injustice of the laws which treat women as inferior to men. The result, she says, is to make women hypocrites and their lives arid. In the lower classes, woman is a servant—in the upper a gracious, frivolous slave. Woman is expected to have two virtues—both contrary to nature—chastity and resignation; and as both those virtues are unnatural she is early taught to deceive. She is forced to become a coquette, seeking to inspire love without sharing it, exciting passion without satisfying it. In forbidding divorce the law claims for human beings what is a prerogative of God. He is permanent, but men and women change. If men's and women's characters always remained the same, there might be reason in requiring the marriage tie to be unbreakable. But one or the other may so change that you may find yourself married to a person entirely different from the one with whom you entered into the marriage pact.

Two years later she published her Esquisses morales, a collection of moral reflections somewhat similar to the Thoughts of Marcus Aurelius. Emerson liked this book so much that when he was in Paris he went to see her that he might express in person his admiration for her ideas. The truth is, the Esquisses gave her opportunity to reveal her character better than any other of her writings. She was essentially a moralist, and even when her passion was most exuberant it was always mingled with a strain of serious reflection.

Neither of these books brought financial reward, but they led to her becoming intimate with advanced thinkers and to her acquiring an interest in politics. "I was thrilled," she says, "by the idea of a republic, but I was never a fanatic. I had neither the traditions nor the language of those who favored a republic. I loved the hierarchy. My sentiments were for the humble, for the popular virtues, for peasants, for working people; but I had no illusions about the character of their work." Holding such views, she lived through the revolution of 1848 with conflicting emotions and after it was over she published a detailed history of its causes. This book was considered by her contemporaries as her chief literary performance. Her later works were a drama, Jeanne d'Arc, another on Marie Stuart, another on Jacques Cœur—none of them very important—and an imaginary dialogue between Goethe and Dante. Along with these she contributed articles to the literary journals, chiefly on matters of art.

During all these years of literary activity Marie seldom spoke of Liszt. The three children she had borne him were taken from her and grew up under the artistic surroundings of their famous sire. Both of the daughters married in Germany, one becoming the wife of the great composer, Richard Wagner. The days which Marie had spent with Liszt came more and more to stand out in her memory as a glorious dream. Her friends made no allusion to him, though they were all aware he continued to be the main object of her thoughts. One only could not be excluded from the tragedy —the person who had been most intimately associated with their love. That person, of course, was George Sand.

When Marie came back to Paris in 1839 her first thought had been to seek the companionship of Sand. That they were both the objects of scandal gave them a common tie, and Sand's fortitude in braving contumely gave Marie hope that she, too, might bear aloft her head. She realized perfectly that the enthusiasm with which their friendship had started could not be renewed. At their last sojourn together at Nohant they had begun to tire of each other, and, though they corresponded after Marie went to Italy, the letters gradually grew more rare. They still indulged in terms of endearment, but it had grown clear to both of them that their hearts were no longer beating in unison. Marie had begun to bore Sand by her constant idealization of love, not very welcome when Sand was embarking on another adventure—this time with Chopin whom Marie had introduced to her. In a moment of exasperation Marie had hinted to a woman friend that she was indignant at the light-hearted manner in which Sand passed from one lover to another. Marie's animadversions were carried to Sand's ears, and, though it must be admitted she had grown a little callous to such charges, it angered her to have such charges uttered by a friend. The correspondence between them ceased, and in March, 1839, Sand wrote to a friend, "I don't know on what foot to dance with her. I have owed her a letter for six or eight months." A month or so later she had fully made up her mind. "I shall not write to madame d'Agoult," she says, "I am not in the habit of making a semblance of friendship. I shall always be ready to serve her and oblige her, for I think she is unhappy. But you may be sure I shall never be effusive."

Marie probably did not realize how deep was Sand's resentment, for in June, 1839, she wrote to Sand asking her to come and visit her in Italy. Sand did not go. In fact, she never received the letter. But her feelings were expressed in a letter which she wrote to a friend in September, 1839. "I have absolutely decided to end all friendly relations with this disagreeable, ungrateful, and false person. She charges Chopin, the friend of Liszt, with having detached me from herself and Liszt." Sand added, however, that Marie was admirable in a rôle of dignity; that she was infinitely intelligent, gracious, and a good companion; that her conversation and manners were seductive and made people love her until they knew her.

Such being Sand's sentiments, Marie's efforts to renew their friendship came, of course, to naught. It never could have been permanent anyway. Their natures were entirely different. It has been truly said that Sand had a genius for love, but no capacity to hold her lovers. Her love was always subjective rather than objective. It was nothing but her extraordinary emotional vitality that made her seek lovers. She once said that she could not conceive how anyone could get along without love. In describing her relations with Chopin she declared, "We did not deceive each other, we simply yielded to the blast which rushed by, carrying us both to some other than an earthly region for a few moments. But it was none the less necessary to alight on solid ground again after the heavenly meeting of our lips and that flight into the empyrean. We poor birds have wings, but our nests are on the ground, and when the voices of the angelic hosts call us aloft the cries of our families tie us to the earth. I have no wish to abandon myself to passion though there is a furnace smouldering in my heart which at times is overpowering."

Unlike Marie, Sand had been educated from childhood to defy conventions. She cared nothing about public opinion, and claimed the right to conduct her private life in any way she chose. Sincere, as she always was, she never expected that her love would last, or at any rate that it would not be interrupted by developments which she could not control.

All this was utterly incomprehensible to Marie. She regarded love as an inspiration from on high, permanent as the source from which it came. So that, much as she admired Sand's genius, and eager as she was to get Sand's literary help, she came in time to see that the gap between them was too wide for her to close. In fact, it grew wider with the growth of time. After Marie's salon became securely established she made a protégée of Juliette Lamber, a talented young woman who was striving to become a writer and who tried her best to smooth the troubled waters. She found it impossible. Marie said to her, "George Sand's lovers are to her a piece of chalk with which she scratches on the blackboard. When she has finished she crushes the chalk under her foot and there remains nothing but the dust which she sweeps away." She also told Juliette that she had given her whole life and soul to Liszt and Sand had tried to steal him away. Whether this was so is hard to say, but at any rate he was a close friend of Sand long after he had passed out of Marie's life. In 1850 Sand wrote, "He was my friend, but he has never been my master."

Bitter as was Marie's animosity, she was always eager to

recognize literary skill, and she prefaced her novel Julien with a dedication to Sand which closed with these words: "We have wanted to love each other." Twenty years later she wrote to Sand a conciliatory letter, and Sand replied, "Thanks for the few words from you, my dear Marie. It is very nice of you to want to complete the happiness of these days for me by adding to it a memory of you, and your congratulations. When one has once really been fond of a person, he never leaves off caring even during long years when it seems that the affection has been forgotten. I no longer remember very well what happened to part us. I live in the present always now, and in my heart to-day you would find nothing which could grieve or disturb you."

In spite of the fundamental difference between these women, they had enough in common to cause some people to regard them as the product of a single mould. Long after they had parted company a distinguished writer of morals published a book denouncing their views of matrimony and pointing to their conduct as a national disgrace. To view the matter in any other light is, of course, impossible. Marie's reticence through all the period of her salon makes it clear she could not offer any just excuse. All she could do was to bear in silence the punishment for her escapade. As Sand said, she was an unhappy woman. Her tastes were always in conflict with her thoughts. By nature an aristocrat, her intellectual processes made of her a democrat.

When the shadows were lengthening she jotted down under

the heading of "Last Thoughts" an analysis of the emotions that had wrecked her life. She says her nature was composed of two irreconcilable elements—an intellectual thirst to know everything and an imperious need of loving and of being loved. Perhaps that was as good a characterization as she could think of to account for the incongruity of her acts.

JULIETTE LAMBER

✗

WITH Juliette Lamber we come down almost to the present day. While still a child she aspired to literary fame, and to the end of her long career there was charm in everything she wrote. But she will be remembered chiefly for her influence in shaping the politics of France.

*

1860's - 1900

LA GRANDE FRANÇAISE, as one of her contemporaries called her, was born in the days of Louis-Philippe and died toward the close of the World War. She lived through four revolutions and saw her country invaded twice. She was a valiant patriot during the siege of Paris, and was all her life a leading advocate of the establishment of the French republic. Her talent as a writer and her fascinating personality brought her into intimate relations with all the great personages of her day and enabled her to exert an influence on politics and literature more effective than that of any other woman of her times.

JULIETTE LAMBER

Her father was a physician in a little town of Picardie, but she was brought up by her maternal grandmother, a woman of determined character between whom and the child's father there was constant strife. Juliette grew up, therefore, in an atmosphere of controversy which kept her mind alert. While her father was pouring into her ears a denunciation of the monarchy, in the eyes of her grandmother democratic notions were at the root of every evil. As to literature her grandmother spent most of her time reading novels of the day. Her father, on the other hand, could see no merit in any writings that did not come from ancient Greece. Which of her advisers contributed chiefly to formulate her principles it would be hard to say. As she grew up she came more and more to share her father's enthusiasm for the democracy of ancient Greece. On the other hand, her grandmother's influence kindled in her a strong liking for the modern writers of romance.

When she was sixteen her grandmother selected for her a husband whom she abhorred. He was a Parisian lawyer of rather meager attainments who dazzled them all with the prospect of giving them a foothold in the great metropolis. That turned out later to be nothing but a bait, and the first three years of Juliette's married life were spent in Soissons.

These three years gave Juliette opportunity to test her literary skill. It was a period when women were coming to be recognized in the intellectual world, and she was eager to become an active participant in that movement. So far as we can detect, there was no thought at that time of interesting herself in politics. It seemed to her that her talent lay in the line of imaginative writing. Like most young persons ambitious to shine in literature, she seems to have spent much of her time in scribbling verses, but only one of her poems, it appears, got into print.

Not till after she took up her abode in Paris did she think seriously of literature as a means of livelihood. It came about in this way. A contributor to one of the periodicals had declared that there was not a pretty woman in France who didn't use crinoline. As she had never adopted the prevailing style she addressed a letter to the publisher in which she informed him that there was one of his readers who could truthfully challenge the contributor's assertion; and she went on to deny the aspersions that had been directed against her sex. The letter, bearing the signature "Juliette," was printed in full. Her heart was filled with pride and in her joy she cried out, "Grandmother, I shall be a writer."

Still pursuing her flair for poetry she now joined a club of poets where the members gathered frequently to listen to the reading of the members' verses, and through the influence of this club she met the famous Béranger. He took a fatherly interest in her and read some of the things she had composed. But he could see nothing in what she showed him to justify high praise and he told her frankly he thought she was pursuing an idle dream. "You will never be a poet," he said, "though you may some day become a writer."

Two years later occurred the event which brought her into relations with George Sand and Marie d'Agoult and placed her permanently in the ranks of those who were fighting for the extension of women's rights. When Proudhon published his book denouncing the two women whom Juliette admired more than any others of her sex, he had the effrontery to call it La justice dans la révolution et dans l'église. He could have used no phrase more suited to kindle Juliette's ire. Justice was the very thing, in her opinion, which women did not have. She determined to compose a refutation of Proudhon's arguments and to use his perverted sense of justice as the basis of her reply.

In this book, the first that came from Juliette's pen, we see the same quality of vigorous argument that is found in all her subsequent writings. Though only twenty-two, she had made up her mind on certain problems, and so far as those problems were concerned her convictions were so firm that no amount of argument could make her waver.

In championing the cause of women her views were not subversive of the existing order. She was not a militant advocate of woman suffrage. Her thought was directed mainly to increasing the individuality of her sex. Proudhon's error, as she saw it, was that he placed too high a value on brute strength. History showed, in her opinion, that civilization was not dependent wholly on the use of force. It was through intellect chiefly that the world progressed and there was no sufficient evidence that women were inferior in intellect to men. That women had not excelled as intellectual leaders was merely because they had been given no encouragement to work. The learned professions should be open to them.

They should be given opportunity to exert an influence on public affairs.

Juliette's little book on woman's right to recognition brought her some favorable comment from the press, but the main benefit which she derived was that it gave her access to the salon of Marie d'Agoult. Twenty years had passed since that great lady had renounced the folly of her youth. Her stately salon had become the place where all the advanced thinkers of the Second Empire were wont to gather. At these meetings all shades of thought were represented, and discussions covered a wide range. Much of the discussion was on politics, a subject on which the "little girl from the country," as she called herself, had not yet formulated her ideas. But she listened with rapture to all the great men had to say. In later years, when politics had become the central feature of her life, she looked back to these discussions as the source of all her inspiration.

Meantime her natural impulses were carrying her along another path. She had not yet reached the time of life when she could get real sustenance in the learned atmosphere of Marie's salon. Paris at that period was at the acme of its fête galante, and Juliette with her lovely face and buoyant spirit soon found herself in a whirl of gayety. One of her intimates was a retired actress who had once been hailed as a rival of the great Rachel. Together these two women were constant frequenters of the theater. One evening she went to a fashionable ball and made so deep an impression on the famous Meyerbeer that for several months he sent a bouquet of violets to her every day. That may have been wholly a bit of gallantry but Juliette was passionately fond of music and it is possible that the great composer thought he detected in her a talent kindred to his own.

All this was not merely the exuberance of youth. She loved people, and had an extraordinary aptitude for making friends. The death of her grandparents shortly after her marriage had provided her with a modest income which enabled her to live in moderate comfort. She had a daughter Alice, born about fifteen months after her marriage, and she would have been genuinely happy but for the constant dissensions between herself and her domineering, pettifogging husband.

In spite of the multiplicity of her social engagements she did not let herself be led away from her ambition to be a writer. In 1860 she published two books under the pseudonym which she used throughout her life. Her maiden name was Lambert and she simply dropped the final letter, calling herself Juliette Lamber. Of these two books one was entitled Mon village. The idea, as well as the name, was suggested by George Sand. It consisted of imaginary dialogues among the people of the little town in Picardie where her father lived. While it gives a faithful picture of the joys and sorrows of simple folk, she wove into their conversations a bit of sound philosophy which she had acquired through close association with village people. The other book, Le mandarin, is an amusing sketch of a Chinaman's experiences in Paris, and it gave the writer a chance to poke fun at some of the incongruities of Parisian life.

The revenue from these books her husband insisted on appropriating to himself. Under the French law he had that right, but Juliette was so indignant at his selfishness that she determined to leave him and went with her daughter to live in the little town where she had been brought up and where her parents now resided. In 1867 her husband died, after they had been separated seven years.

Her next literary venture was her Récits d'une paysanne, published in 1862. Nothing that she had hitherto written exhibited her qualities better than this little book. It is a collection of stories about peasant children and it gives abundant evidence of the writer's kindly heart, of her joyous spirit, and of her genuine interest in the tastes and feelings of humble people. One would never suspect in perusing these tales of peasant life that the author had just come from the fashionable circles of Parisian society.

In the midst of this literary work she was suddenly taken ill. The doctors thought she was threatened with pulmonary consumption and ordered her to spend the winter at Cannes. At first she did not like Cannes but after a while she enjoyed it so much that in the following winter she persuaded her father to buy a little plot of ground at Golfe-Juan and build her a villa there. This villa she called The Briars, and it continued for many years to be her winter home. It was here, in 1863, that she wrote her little sketch, Autour du Grand-Pin.

In 1864, on the suggestion of Marie d'Agoult, she estab-

lished her first salon in Paris. Marie told her, and no one
better than Marie could advise, that to establish a salon she
must have at her beck and call twenty men and five women—a
number that Juliette easily could command. Other instructions were to combine simplicity with elegance, to appear
serene and confident, and to let those whom she had gathered
around her feel that responsibility for the salon's success
depended on them. Juliette's was to be the little summer salon
when the grand salon of Marie was closed. And so Juliette
came back to Paris, and opened her salon in the rue de
Rivoli, choosing that site, as she jocosely tells us, because it
was in the rue de Rivoli that all revolutions had their birth.

In 1868, one year after the death of her first husband,
she married Edmond Adam, a banker and stanch republican, several years her senior, whom she called "the
chivalrous Adam." His infatuation had begun six years
earlier, when he first saw her at a concert and asked to be
introduced. Having recently separated from her husband she
resented his attentions and withdrew from the room. When
her book Mon village came out, he wrote and offered his
congratulations, to which she returned a cold reply. But he
was not to be discouraged. He let no opportunity escape to
win her affections, and in the end prevailed. On the day after
she learned of her husband's death they became engaged.
Marie d'Agoult attempted to dissuade her. "An intelligent
woman," she said, "should remain free and mistress of her
own thoughts." "But I have greater need of happiness than

of freedom," replied Juliette. This was the end of the friendship between these self-willed women—a sad ending to a communion which had meant so much to both of them.

So far as Juliette was concerned, her marriage to Edmond Adam brought into her life nothing but happiness. He proved to be a man of unswerving patriotism as well as a devoted husband. It was not so much love as admiration that held them together. She always addressed him as Adam and felt unbounded respect for his ideals. In return he appreciated the brilliancy of her mind and the accuracy of her judgment. Immediately after their marriage he begged her to give up The Briars and live at his villa Le Grand-Pin which was near by. He said he did not want to be known as monsieur Lamber. But he finally yielded and said to her he could understand that she did not want to give up a house which was built by her personal effort and come and live in one which was built only by his money. When they returned to Paris, however, she yielded to his wishes and moved her salon from the rue de Rivoli to the boulevard Poissonnière, and established herself in the Maison Sallandrouze which was directly opposite his favorite café.

During all the years of Juliette's intimacy with Marie d'Agoult she had kept up an earnest correspondence with George Sand, but they had never met face to face. With laudable self-denial Sand had refused to establish a friendship with her youthful admirer lest such action should stand in the way of Juliette's intimacy with Marie. That impediment was now removed, and Juliette hastened to grasp the happiness for which she had been longing ever since she wrote her eulogy of Sand. They met at Sand's apartment and sealed a bond of friendship which lasted till the famous novelist was carried to the grave. It was an alliance of two persons totally different in character but whose ideals were the same. Juliette was an avowed pagan. Sand claimed to be a believer in the national faith. But both were worshippers of nature, unfettered by tradition, lovers of the beautiful. That was enough to hold them together in spite of the diversity in their modes of life.

Juliette has left us a graphic picture of their first meeting. When their intimacy began, Sand had reached the age of sixty-three. Her turbulent days were over. Instead of daring romances she was writing stories of peasant life. From a literary standpoint she and Juliette were plowing in the same field. It was Sand who had put into Juliette's mind the idea of Mon village. So when Juliette made her first call on Sand she was confident they would prove to be kindred spirits. She was not mistaken. Her heart throbbed with excitement as she entered Sand's apartment. Sand was sitting at her table rolling a cigarette. She did not rise but motioned to Juliette to be seated. Neither of them spoke, and Juliette was so overcome with emotion that she burst into tears. Sand threw her arms around her young visitor, who opened the conversation by recounting the story of her breach with Marie d'Agoult. Sand ejaculated that it was incomprehensible.

A few days later they went together to the theater, after

which Sand asked Juliette to accompany her to her apartment and have a talk. "I want my life to be of service to you, my adopted child," she said. And she gave that night a more detailed explanation of her strange career than is to be found in anything else that is recorded. "I have accepted love as it came to me, but have never sought it. . . . In my youth I lived in an artificial world where everyone was the echo of everyone else, when all wanted to feel, love, and think differently from the common people. We lost our foothold in striving to swim where the water was too deep. . . . To-day, my child, the life which I and the men of my generation lived is no longer possible. There is left no trace of the artistic caste which succeeded the military caste and which in turn succeeded the aristocratic caste. . . . Mingling with the masses, men have lost our foolish passion for ideals. They suffer less than we did, for they have fewer illusions. . . . Are they happier than we were? I cannot say. But our chief fault was that we allowed sensuality to enter into our striving for the ideal."

This talk made a deep impression on Juliette. "From that evening," she says, "my great maternal friend has been my guide."

In the winter of 1868 her "great friend" stayed with her for a month at The Briars. There Sand was at her best. All her good traits stood out. As Juliette said, "To live with George Sand was to realize how simple she was, always satisfied, always thinking of others, never letting one suspect she was tired or had a care." Juliette's husband had given her a yacht for New Year's and they all revelled in lying on its deck and basking in the sun. Sand called Adam "bow wow" which she considered a compliment, for she adored canines. "The next best animal to a dog is a man," she used to say. They spent much time picking flowers, which was Sand's chief hobby.

Sand's genuineness, her kindly nature, her sympathy, were so patent that persons admitted to her intimacy always tried to minimize her faults. To Juliette her "great friend" was almost without a blemish. It was not love, it was a desire to comfort, that led to her indiscretions with Alfred de Musset, with Chopin, with Mérimée. "George Sand's capacity for love was not wholly passion. As a friend she has always shown fidelity, a kindliness, a devotion, which her lovers have never found in any other woman. . . . What she considered passion was a composite of sentiments wholly foreign to transports of the heart and senses." Her final judgment was summed up in these words written after Sand was dead: "Great, great friend, I shall ever hold as friends those who love you, who honor, praise, and admire you; and as enemies those who, guilty of greater faults than yours, accuse you."

Not long after Juliette's marriage Sand rented an apartment in Paris and Juliette saw her "grande amie" almost every day. Juliette was engaged at this time in writing two novels, L'Éducation de Laure, and Saine et sauve, in both of which it is easy to trace the influence of Sand. Neither of them can be ranked as a work of genius, though they gave abundant proof of the author's facile pen.

L'Éducation de Laure, published in 1868, was really a recital of her own education. It proves, if any proof be needed, that all her training tended to make her oblivious of the realities of life. She was brought up in a world of abstractions which gave a false color to all her later life. This education led her into a wholly undue admiration of the ancient Greeks and all their civilization stood for. You can see this error in a series of articles on contemporary Greek poetry which she wrote many years later for La nouvelle revue. She saw in that poetry a beauty of form and substance which no one, with the exception perhaps of Byron, had been able to discover. She was so charming a companion, and her loyalty and joyousness were so pervasive, that her zeal for Hellenism did not materially affect her social relations, though many of her friends tried to turn her thoughts into more rational channels. Marie d'Agoult told her she was too young and beautiful to waste her time on Aristotle and Plato. George Sand treated Juliette's Hellenism as a joke, and Adam, much as he adored his wife, went into the next room when she insisted on discussing Greek philosophy.

The truth is, Juliette was now entering upon a new field of activity in which she was destined to acquire lasting fame. She was coming to be an active participant in public affairs.

The Maison Sallandrouze was generally recognized as the rallying place of those opposed to the imperial form of government established by Napoleon III. Edmond Adam had been one of the most ardent republicans of 1848, and he had never ceased to denounce the coup d'état by which France had once more become an empire. So bitter was his opposition to the empire that he refused to hold any office that required him to swear allegiance to the existing government, and the doors of his hospitable home were always thrown wide open to all who clamored for a republic. Of such, the most vociferous was a young lawyer from the south of France named Léon Gambetta. Though of exceedingly humble origin, and speaking the French language with an accent that grated on Parisian ears, by his skill as an orator he had gained a great ascendency over the common people. So it occurred to Adam that he might be a useful ally, and he suggested to Juliette that she invite Gambetta to one of her elaborate dinners. At first the idea of having him at her house caused her a good deal of trepidation. Some of her friends told her it was impossible. They called him a monster, a man of coarse texture, unsuitable in every way to sit at her table. Still, she realized that the very traits that would be repulsive to her guests were invaluable in promoting the cause which she and her husband had so close to their hearts. She decided to try the experiment.

Gambetta came in rough attire, with soft collar and flannel shirt. Apparently he knew nothing of social customs and when he was presented to his hostess he mumbled, "If I had known ——" She finished his sentence for him, "You would not have come, and that would not have been nice of you." To put him at ease she insisted on his taking her in to dinner and sitting on her right.

A few days later he was employed to defend a distin-

guished citizen arrested for advocating a memorial to one
of the revolutionists who had been killed in 1848. The
accused was convicted, but Gambetta's eloquence thrilled the
crowds that packed the courtroom. Instead of presenting evidence for the defendant he launched into a bitter denunciation of the government. The authorities were speechless with
indignation, and the opposition was beside itself with joy.
"We have found our leader," they were all saying. He had
an uncanny talent, according to Juliette, in sensing public
opinion and expressing it in concrete form. Juliette and her
husband were too uncompromising to approve entirely of
Gambetta's methods, but they were so wedded to the idea of
a republic that they came to lean on him more than on any
other man in public life.

It was now becoming clear to everyone that war with Germany was at hand. The great material prosperity that France
had enjoyed for a generation made her a tempting prize.
With blind confidence in his military prowess Napoleon III
had treated the threatening warfare with unconcern. He
had counted on Italy and Austria to stand with France if
any outbreak should occur. In spite of constant warnings that
Prussia was raising a formidable army, he made no effort
to secure the services of capable generals and allowed his
military organization to fall into disarray. So great was the
discontent with his administration that he did not dare to
burden the nation with increased expenditure for armament.
To admit that France was in danger of invasion he was well
aware would lead to revolution. The best policy, as he con-

ceived it, was to put on a bold front and in case of necessity declare war on Prussia before she was ready to attack.

On July 19th, 1870, the mad adventure started with a declaration of war by France. Napoleon III left Paris to take command of his army, 350,000 strong. The Germans, with 520,000 men, joined battle all along the front, winning virtually every engagement. On September 2nd Mac-Mahon was routed at Sedan, and 104,000 men, including Napoleon, became prisoners of war.

These dreadful tidings came to Juliette at the Maison Sallandrouze. She rushed into the street, which was packed with vociferous men and women giving voice to their indignation. Napoleon the Little, as he was called, was almost forgotten in the people's wrath at the corps législatif which had voted for this stupid war. Juliette allowed herself to be carried along by the mob. Everyone was shouting for the dissolution of the government. Here and there crowds were gathered around a fiery orator urging an attack on the chambre des députés. Those who had long been seeking to overthrow the government believed their hour of victory was at hand. As night fell, the crowds grew thinner and by one o'clock in the morning most people had returned to their homes. "It is in the family," writes Juliette, "that the nation holds its final council. The lights in the houses announce not a festival but a wake—a wake of tears. Under every roof is an invalid in his last extremity with all the family at his bedside. The invalid is France in her last agony."

The next morning, in accordance with arrangements made

the night before by the leaders of the opposition, the garde nationale wearing their uniforms but without their guns gathered in the place de la Concorde, and the people rallied about them, determined to force their way into the chambre. Juliette pushed her way into the crowd and made a speech— her first speech in public, she declares. "The republic," she said, "is the greatest product of our courage, intelligence, activity, growth. If society is an enlarged replica of ourselves, the republic is the result of our best deeds, it is a living composite of our largest duties, rights, and interests. Republics are not decreed, they are made. No social malady, no monarchical cancer, shall again kill it. Vive la république!"

When the crowds reached the chambre they found that most of the deputies had fled. Gambetta, who was one of the few to remain, jumped to his feet and shouted, "Bonaparte and his dynasty have forever ceased to reign in France." It was then agreed that the deputies from Paris should proceed to the hôtel de ville and constitute themselves le gouvernement de la défense nationale.

So, without the shedding of a drop of blood, emerged the republic which Juliette had so many years espoused. "Henceforth," she wrote in her journal, "it is for France and not for a dynasty that we shall fight. It is for our country that we shall be patriots."

Everyone expected that the next step would be an attack on Paris. All of the regular army except the troops shut up in the fortresses at Metz and Belfort had been annihilated.

Nothing stood in the way of the Prussi march on Paris. Many people thought it folly to resist Not so, Juliette. "I am for battle," she wrote in her journal. Paris was surrounded on all sides by forts and so long as they held firm the city was safe from the enemy's artillery. To man the forts an urgent call was sent to the marines, the only armed men left who knew how to handle heavy guns. The garde mobile, consisting chiefly of peasants, was brought hastily to the capital, and it formed the nucleus of a new army. In addition there was the garde nationale composed of clerks and shopkeepers, well intentioned but having no real knowledge of military affairs. All able-bodied men were urged to volunteer. Juliette's husband joined the garde nationale as a private soldier.

Most of the women and all of the diplomatic corps except the American minister departed. Juliette determined to stay and see it through. There was much opposition to the new government which had assumed control and Juliette felt it her duty to use such influence as she had to strengthen its position. "We must not leave them, we must second, advise, and sustain them."

In less than a week the Prussians had surrounded the city and had begun the siege. With pardonable foresight Juliette busied herself with laying up provisions. How long the city would hold out no one knew. Some said two weeks. Others, including Juliette, guessed three months.

What could she do to help? In each ward was established a hospital for the wounded. As daughter of a physician and granddaughter of a surgeon, she felt it specially appropriate that she take part in this work. She volunteered to organize a hospital with thirty beds. Her offer was accepted and the conservatoire de musique was turned over to her for the purpose. Here she worked all day long making bandages and preparing medicines to be ready for the wounded as they came in. When the day's work was over she sat down and wrote letters to everybody she could think of, begging for money for her hospital.

The city was still in touch with the outside world by underground telegraph wires. Reports came in that the provinces were recruiting armies to come to the relief of Paris. Juliette had little confidence in these reports. She says in her journal, "In the privacy of my own home I doubt, but when I go out I express faith. Men get their strength by confidence, women by trusting in the heavens." What was needed, it seemed to her, was a man of force to stir the provinces into action, and she hailed with eagerness the plan which Adam favored of having Gambetta cross the lines in a balloon and employ his eloquence to arouse the people. This plan was put into effect on October 7th, and met with some success, though the armies which Gambetta recruited were never able to reach Paris.

As the days passed without any improvement in the situation, Juliette grew impatient. She distrusted the capacity of the commander of the besieged city. "The main thing is not to shut our forces up in Paris. We should harass the enemy. Every day, every night, we should throw our men of valor upon the enemy's camps so as to spread terror and alarm among them."

The communists were now beginning to give trouble in the outskirts of Paris. The government asked Adam to accept the office of prefect of police. "You tell me," said Adam, "it is a dangerous post and requires a devoted patriot. Very well, I don't care to think it over. I accept." Juliette was in despair. She admired his courage, but considered him too outspoken for a position which required so many clandestine negotiations. However, she went with him to live in the prefect's offices—"a horrible prison," she calls it. Her friends had begged Adam to accept this position and now none of her friends would even come to see her. She was right in her estimate of Adam as prefect of police. In spite of all he could do, the communists got out of hand. Adam went to the commander of the army and begged that a marine officer be appointed to keep the people quiet, as they had more respect for the marines than for the garde nationale. Nothing came of his suggestion and the communists grew bolder. One had to be always on the alert, said Juliette. "If in an hour of danger the prefect must pay with his body Adam will be ready to pay."

The improvised army made a few feeble sorties but was always defeated. The people were growing more and more exasperated. They blamed the generals, most of whom were left-overs from the empire. On October 30th, public opinion had become so threatening that Adam did not go to bed all night. People were denouncing le gouvernement de la défense nationale so vigorously that he expected at any minute to learn of an attack on the hôtel de ville. The next morning he ordered twenty battalions of the garde nationale to be in readiness to resist the attack. A little after one o'clock he went to the hôtel de ville. Crowds began to gather demanding an election to replace the provisional government. Before nightfall the crowd had forced its way into the hôtel de ville and arrested all members of the government, including Adam. Juliette heard the news in the prefecture. Suddenly, at half past six, Adam appeared and gave orders that the prefecture be defended. Then he rushed back to the hôtel de ville. Juliette was left alone in the prefecture. She was advised to pull down the window shades, but she refused and kept all the lights lit to let the populace know that business was being conducted as usual.

As the garde nationale which Adam had ordered to proceed to the hôtel de ville had not obeyed, he went to the place Vendôme for an explanation. The lieutenant-colonel replied that he had given the order but the troops had slunk off on the way. But he would see that the order was carried out between nine and ten.

In the evening an officer came to the prefecture to take possession and showed Juliette a paper announcing that Adam had been removed by the government. She did not believe it and refused to give up the prefecture. While the officers of the prefecture were still holding out, news arrived that Adam had gone to the hôtel de ville about midnight under escort of the garde mobile and the garde nationale. Entering by a secret passage, he found the whole building packed with insurgents, many of them carrying guns. All the members of the government were there and Adam joined them. It was a threatening mob that the government had to face. After bickering till nearly dawn it was agreed that the mob should disperse but that an election should be held the same day and the people given the right to choose a new government. At half past five the hôtel de ville had been cleared of the mob and Adam went back to the prefecture, where he found Juliette waiting for him. She had been sitting up all night.

He was awakened after a few minutes' sleep by an officer from the government demanding the arrest of the leaders of the insurgents. Adam informed them that it had been agreed as one of the conditions of the mob's withdrawal that none of their leaders should be arrested. This the agent denied and Adam was ordered to get out of bed and present himself at the hôtel de ville. He complied and told the members of the government frankly that the agreement though only verbal had been distinctly that there would be no arrests. He refused to go back on his word. As the government did not agree with him, he insisted on resigning his post as prefect of police. It was a delicate situation. No one questioned Adam's sincerity, but some of the members of the government were not entirely clear in their memory of what had been said. They felt it would encourage further disorders if they allowed the ringleaders to escape punishment. Finally they accepted Adam's resignation, and he gave up his post, much to the relief of Juliette.

When Metz fell, 200,000 more Prussian soldiers were left free to attack Paris. The question at once arose whether it would not be wise to seek an armistice. The government finally voted against it. Juliette was overjoyed. "We must cling to our sublime folly as a precious jewel." When the enemy's bombs began to fall in the city she wrote, "I would give my house and a hundred others in order to hold out two days longer." . . . "I must encourage by my optimism those who have less hope than I have. Women cannot fight. Their duty is to strengthen the courage of those who can."

On November 24th she was shown a letter from Gambetta saying he had recruited an army of 200,000 men and was to have 100,000 more in eight days. "At last! Vive la France! She will live then, our country. No one will trample her under foot. We shall find Frenchmen to defend her. . . . All Paris owes a debt of gratitude to Gambetta."

On December 11th she writes, "I am suffering terribly from rheumatism. For nine years I have passed four months of each year at Golfe-Juan. I have never known cold more than one degree below zero, centigrade. Last night it was fifteen below in my bedroom." She was forced by ill health to resign as head of her ambulance corps. Eggs were now selling at 2 francs apiece, butter 28 francs a pound, rabbits 40 francs apiece, chickens 25 to 50, turkeys and geese 100 to 200. When she invited friends to dinner, each was expected to bring food with him. Hers was virtually gone. And she was without wood to heat her apartment. Everyone was using his chairs and tables as firewood, and the government was cutting down all the trees in the streets.

On January 5th Juliette with other ladies opened a sale at one of the railway stations in aid of working women. Juliette had a kiosk where she sold newspapers and periodicals.

The city was now being bombarded, and old men, women, and children were being killed.

On January 19th the garde nationale made another sortie, but without avail. They were driven back with heavy loss, and the commander of the Parisian troops made an announcement that he had asked for a two-days armistice. It was none too soon. People were dying of starvation all over the city. Two weeks more and there would not have been a scrap of food left. The armistice was granted, and before the two days were over Paris had capitulated.

The armistice signed, Juliette could not restrain her indignation at its terms. Bismarck had insisted that an assemblée be elected to agree upon the terms of peace, and she believed that an assemblée elected while foreign armies were in control could not represent the real interests of the people. She was pleased, however, when Adam was elected one of the delegates from Paris.

When the delegates came together Bismarck announced his terms—the cession of Alsace excepting Belfort, also a part of Lorraine including Metz, an indemnity of five billion francs, the entry into Paris on March 1st of 30,000 Prussian soldiers who were to bivouac in the place de la Concorde till ratifications should be exchanged, and the fortresses along the eastern frontier to remain in the enemy's hands until the indemnity was paid. On learning of these humiliating terms, Juliette exclaimed, "They have torn out the heart of France." Gambetta arose from his seat in the assemblée and pleaded vehemently for a continuance of the war. Being voted down he flew into a rage and resigned his seat in the assemblée. Sand wrote to Adam that Bismarck's terms must be accepted and denounced Gambetta for his opposition. Juliette was shocked by this letter. "An abyss has opened," she declared, "between me and my dearest friend. We do not understand each other."

Then came the rising of the commune in Paris. Adam hurried from Versailles where the assemblée was sitting, and endeavored to calm the communists, but without avail. He returned to Versailles and tried to persuade Thiers, who had been elected chief of the executive power, to conciliate the communists. This also was without avail. Nobody seemed to know exactly what the communists wanted. Some said they were agents of Bismarck, others thought they were being spurred on by Gambetta. The probability is they merely sought an opportunity to plunder. Adam made a point of returning to Paris every night as proof of his desire to conciliate the rabble.

All this time Juliette was at The Briars. She was eager to go to Paris and play her part, but Adam insisted that she stay away. The government at Versailles did not undertake to quell the rioting in Paris. They did not feel secure enough of their position. The army was lukewarm to the new government and would have deserted rather than fire on their fellow-citizens. Adam arranged a meeting between the republican league and the communists but little came of it. After a couple of months, order was restored by troops under Mac-Mahon, and Juliette returned to Paris.

From now on, Juliette threw herself heart and soul into the political affairs of France. For many months after peace was declared the assemblée was struggling to decide what form of government should be established. The assemblée had been elected while the country was in a state of turmoil and before the people had had an opportunity to formulate their plans. Some of the delegates from the very start were in favor of a republic, but the majority, having lived all their lives under a monarchical form of government, were slow to favor any radical change. That the deliberations of the assemblée finally resulted in the establishment of a republic was due in some measure, at least, to the ceaseless energy of Juliette.

Its earliest sessions gave Juliette little cause for hope. Thiers, the presiding officer, and nearly all the members were lukewarm to the idea of a republic. Juliette, who sat as a spectator at almost every session, was terribly distressed to observe that no one of real persuasive power seemed to advocate a republic. She talked it over with Adam, and both agreed there was no chance of setting up a republic unless they could find a brilliant leader to champion their cause.

The ideal man, of course, was Gambetta, but he had lost all
influence through his obstinate refusal to sign the treaty with
Germany. In Juliette's eyes that was no ground for reproach,
though nearly all her friends regarded Gambetta's action as
the height of folly. The upshot of it was that Adam finally
wrote to Gambetta and begged him to take his seat once more
in the assemblée. Gambetta yielded, and from that day he
and Juliette worked hand in hand to establish the republic.
Juliette was present when Gambetta made his first speech in
the assemblée at Versailles. She was already acquainted with
his extraordinary power to sway his audiences, but she did
not know him intimately enough to be sure of the real sentiments that lay beneath his persuasive eloquence. Some people
spoke of him as a "fiery madman" and it piqued her curiosity
to see whether he was inspired by true patriotism or was
merely a charlatan seeking public applause. She came away a
little disappointed. She describes him as fat, heavy, badly
dressed, shuffling along rather than walking. With his large
head and shaggy hair he reminded her of a lion. His address
seemed to her surprisingly undemonstrative. She had expected
to hear him launch forth into a violent attack upon Thiers
for his monarchical ideas.

The fact was, of course, that Gambetta, with his uncanny
skill at sensing the feelings of his hearers, saw at a glance
that the time was not ripe for a vehement attack. He must
wait until his unpopularity in the assemblée had worn off.
Adam, who had far more political sagacity than his wife,
was not altogether disheartened. He had been all his life on

terms of intimacy with Thiers, and he believed the best way to bring him into the fold was to let republican doctrines filter gradually into his mind.

The Maison Sallandrouze, which had remained quiescent since the beginning of the siege, was now seething with activity again. Those famous Wednesday and Friday dinners were renewed, and among the guests were always to be found the members of the assemblée who favored a republic. Gambetta, now decently equipped by Adam's tailor, was always there, and, as Juliette came to know him better, she grew to have entire confidence in the genuineness of his sentiments. His speeches were winning many adherents, and both Juliette and her husband were looking up to him as their "great leader." With Adam's assistance he established a newspaper to disseminate his political principles. When the project was being started Juliette declared, "The office of the République will be in the rue de Croissant, but its salon will be in the Maison Sallandrouze." Egotistical as that may seem, no one could deny that the deputies were coming more and more to sympathize with the policies which were being shaped beneath her roof. It was a tedious process. Five years were used up in deliberations, but in the end the republic was set firmly on its feet.

Through these five years the hostess of the Maison Sallandrouze was in almost daily association with Gambetta. Their views did not at all times coincide, but the personal affection which had now grown up between them kept them pulling steadily together in the fundamental purpose by which they were equally inspired. As a matter of fact, they were by natural instinct birds of a feather—creatures of sentiment. Gambetta, no less than Juliette, was an idealist. In spite of his uncouth demeanor, he had a delicate appreciation of art. Deep down in his heart was a craving for romantic adventure. He was one of the few persons frequenting her salon who shared her love of the old Greek culture. Whenever Gambetta's strenuous political activity permitted, he found no one to whom he was able to divulge his intimate thoughts so freely as he could with her, and it was in Gambetta more than in any other that she found a sympathetic listener to her literary effusions.

Apart from personal considerations, what cemented their friendship more than anything else was their sentimental advocacy of the "revanche." In summoning to arms the whole French nation within a couple of days after his flight in the balloon from Paris he had exhorted, "Let us rise as one man and die rather than endure the shame of dismemberment." And in an address which he made in 1872, he declared, "If there is one thing that can comfort and strengthen us in our sorrowful mourning for our dismembered country, it is the thought of those good French mothers who will assure to France her champions and avengers." These were brave words to be uttered while the Prussian army was still encamped in France. But they were none too brave for Juliette who in season and out of season was crying for revenge.

The assemblée had been elected at the behest of Bismarck because he refused to admit that le gouvernement de la défense nationale had any power to negotiate terms of peace. Gambetta took the view that the duties of the assemblée had been performed when the treaty of peace was signed. But he was voted down, and the assemblée lasted five years till it had formulated all the terms of the new constitution. Gambetta remained a member till the end and his voice was often heard with interest and applause, though the real effort of his life through those five years was to promulgate his doctrines in the columns of his paper, the République française. Through his influence that paper became not only a financial success, but a tremendous power. The form of constitution finally adopted was the result of the doctrines set forth in that paper and exhibited in no slight degree the impress of Juliette's thoughts.

When he first took his seat in the assemblée, Gambetta was thirty-three. In spite of his unquestioned patriotism, he had emerged from the recent conflict with a damaged reputation. Perhaps it was through no fault of his, but the armies that he had so enthusiastically recruited had gone down in defeat. His following was made up of the most dangerous elements in France. Most respectable people regarded him as a communist. A bachelor, with no pecuniary resources, his only asset of importance was his marvellous forensic ability. Being accepted, therefore, as the protégé of a great banker was like picking up manna from heaven. It enabled him to repair his shattered reputation and to enter on a path in which his talent as an orator was sure to bring success.

He was fortunate, too, in finding that in fundamental doctrines he and the house of Adam were in full accord. In the early days of the assemblée there were two subjects that gave rise to endless discussion. One was the establishment of a powerful army, and the other was the spread of universal education. To accomplish these two purposes Adam as well as Juliette had set their hearts, and Gambetta started by making them the keynotes of his public life.

Strange indeed it would have been if this community of interests had not led to personal intimacy. Gambetta planned to pass a portion of the winter with his friends at The Briars, a project that fell through only because he was confined to his room by gout. "He is showing toward us a constantly growing friendship," comments Juliette. "Our worship of Gambetta increases every day." "We must often have him at The Briars in his vacations." They had a good excuse, for Gambetta's father had taken up his abode in Nice. He called on Juliette and begged her to use her influence with Thiers to secure employment for his nephew. With so great a son he thought his nephew entitled to any post. Thiers at that period distrusted Gambetta, but Adam interceded and the post was secured. Juliette went to Nice with the good news. She found all the family there, father, mother, sister, and a servant who was regarded by all as a member of the family. The sister, whom everybody loved, lacked education but was full of energy and had a brilliant mind. Juliette stayed all day listening with rapture while they sang the praises of "the great statesman."

Juliette went home with the praises of Gambetta ringing

in her ears. The fiery orator had become the embodiment
of her ideals. No one could persuade her that he had a fault.
Sand kept writing to her that Gambetta was using her to
advance his personal interests. "He is a sorcerer," she said.
But Juliette turned a deaf ear to all such warnings. Not long
after, her daughter was married and Gambetta was asked
to serve as one of the two witnesses.

When Thiers fell, he was succeeded as president of the
republic by Mac-Mahon, and Gambetta began to lay his
plans to be appointed president of the council. Juliette was
still looking forward to the "revanche" and planned to discuss
it with Gambetta the next time he came to see her at The
Briars. But there were already indications that he was breaking away. He was making other influential friendships and
did not feel the need of her assistance as he had in the days
of his apprenticeship.

In due time Gambetta came to spend a week at The Briars.
Juliette records that though they agreed in their general
conception regarding the republic, they differed as to many
details. She longed for what she called an Athenian republic,
governed by an aristocracy based on quality, where the best
men should control. Gambetta wanted to raise the masses to
the level of the best. However, they allowed no differences of
opinion to affect their friendship. She found Gambetta a
jolly companion, fond of the good things of life. She had just
published her Récits du Golfe-Juan with which Gambetta
was delighted, and in a moment of confidence she told him
she was not free to write just as she pleased. She had written

a romance called Païenne which she had kept secret from her husband. Gambetta insisted on her reading the manuscript to him. He was enchanted, but they had to put it away when Adam came into the room.

In the autumn of 1874, when she was leaving for The Briars, she begged Gambetta to continue his "conversations" with her by letter. He pleaded that he was a poor letter writer, but he promised to write, as he was still anxious for her to keep him posted about the news which she was able to gather from her numerous friends. The news from Germany was menacing and on that subject she and Gambetta were beginning to draw apart. She wanted France to form an alliance with Russia, while Gambetta believed any steps in that direction would precipitate another invasion of France by Bismarck. In this belief Gambetta was sincere, and without much question right. In the first of the conversations which he had promised he wrote her frankly that France was not in any mood for another war. The capital had again resigned itself to a life of pleasure. This was manifestly written in a moment of depression, for the next day he wrote her again and told her she must not take him too seriously. "I am well aware," he writes, "that my talks with you are not diplomatic, but by telling you my impressions just as they come to me I shall show myself to you as I am, vacillating and changeable. . . . I want to keep you informed not of events but of the impressions they make on me." That he was changeable she had already begun to discern. A few days later he wrote her that Paris was overrun with foreigners—"one of the many symptoms of the crisis which threatens us because of the miserable feebleness of our government." Juliette could not quite see how the weakness of the government had anything to do with the presence of foreigners. Perhaps he did not know himself, but in the course of his rambling comments he threw out an idea which in the light of what happened forty years later looks like prophetic vision. "The slavic world is in a state of fermentation. We may expect that the slightest misadventure in Serbia or Bosnia will set all Europe aflame." He suggested that France ally herself with the Balkans to prevent such a conflagration. Juliette also was for an alliance with the Slavs, but not with the Balkan states. She wanted nothing less than Russia as an ally.

Within a week he was on the top of the wave. The elections which had been going on for the last few days gave his group a great preponderance in the assemblée, and he writes a joyous letter to "Our Lady of The Briars." She had written him that his views were distorted by his constricted association with the journalists and politicians of Paris and that the wider associations which she had made enabled her to take a saner view of the situation. He had to admit his folly in expressing so positively his transitory views. "But," he writes, "my frankness was worth while, for it has brought me this lovely, enthusiastic letter in which I can almost feel the beating of your heart so full of passionate devotion to France. It is only woman who can love her country as you do." She had reached the point now where his arguments had lost their weight, and she detected a note of insincerity when he closed his letter by calling himself her "resident minister in the good City of Paris." However, she was ready to sink all personal animosity for the sake of France. "My duty to our leader is to be sincere with him, to lay aside all personal feeling and to say to him with possibly excessive frankness, in order that it may sink deeper, what I know to be the truth."

The truth was, as Juliette knew, that Gambetta was absolutely indispensable to the cause for which she stood. He was the leader of the opposition, and his untiring energy, his eloquence, his growing reputation as a champion of the masses, enabled him to stir up enthusiasm in the most lethargic departments of France. As Juliette declared, he was the central figure wherever there was a contest. She knew he was an opportunist and she did not like him for it, but he was a master in the art of grouping the divergent influences in the country districts. "He was a general who knew the numbers and the value of his soldiers." As a campaigner he had no equal, and that, for Juliette, was enough to compensate for almost any fault. She continued to write him constantly and saw to it that his abode in Paris was always plentifully supplied with flowers from The Briars.

In the winter of 1875 he paid another visit to her in the course of which he spent a day with his poor old mother at Nice. It was an empty day. Prosperity had turned his head, and he told Juliette he would never go there again. While he was at The Briars, they got to discussing national charac-

teristics. Gambetta declared that the Latin spirit was generous and progressive, that Latin conquests had always brought
life, a sense of legal authority, and order, while the German
spirit was perpetual argument based on alleged superiority
of intellect. "Germany is personified today in Bismarck,
France is personified in me." We have no record of Juliette's
reply, but, whatever she may have thought, it is safe to say
her delicacy of feeling prevented her from making the retort
which he deserved. She never allowed her guests to take
offense, and after he got back to Paris he wrote her that his
visit had strangely fortified his serenity and given him
strength to face the intrigues with which he had to cope.

Down in the south of France he had been working on an
intrigue of his own. His sister Benedetta had lost her husband in the siege of Paris, and had found a refuge in the
family home in Nice. Gambetta had grown tired of contributing to her support and wanted her to find another husband. He had even gone so far as to pick out the man for her
to marry—a man who had long been a friend of Benedetta.
Distrusting his own capacity to negotiate so delicate a business, he had called on Juliette to put it through. With characteristic urbanity she did her best. She called upon the
prospective husband and portrayed in glowing colors, as in
all verity she could, the charming qualities of Benedetta.
It was not a matter to be pressed too hard. But in the end it
came to pass in conformity with her friend's desires.

When the assemblée, after its five years of deliberation,
was preparing to dissolve, Juliette had cause to fear that she

was approaching the most tragic disillusionment of her life. Gambetta had turned his back on Alsace and Lorraine. The constitution adopted, he had given up all thought of the "revanche." His political future had come to be the main object of his thought. She began to suspect that what she had always looked upon as patriotism might in the end turn out to be nothing but a thirst for power. She could hardly believe that possible, but there were moments when the thought caused her bitter anguish. Gambetta realized that he no longer stood so firmly on the pedestal to which Juliette had raised him, and he made a strenuous effort to restore himself to her good graces. He writes her, "You can never know what your help has meant to me, or what an egotist I am in madly loving you." She jots down in her journal that he is using every effort to convince her of his friendship. Adam had been elected one of the seventy-five life senators and it was increasingly important to Gambetta that he keep on good footing with Adam's wife.

In the winter of 1876 Gambetta was again at The Briars, and Juliette read to him the manuscript of her Jean et Pascal. It was the first book which she had written since her marriage without consulting her husband. At an earlier visit Adam had agreed that he would no longer interfere by giving Juliette advice, and would let Gambetta be her only critic. Gambetta was so delighted when she read to him the tender passages about Alsace that he could hardly restrain his emotion. She wondered whether she had not misjudged him in thinking that his interest in foreign politics had robbed him of his love for Alsace. Even Adam was enchanted by the story and promised that he would never again endeavor to clip her wings.

Gambetta was elected a member of the chambre des députés by an imposing majority and was immediately made president of the budget commission, a post which carried with it immense power. He was now considered by many to be the coming man of France, and in September, 1876, he determined to learn at first hand the true condition of affairs in Germany. Shaving off his beard he travelled incognito all through Germany, and was tremendously impressed by the thoroughness with which the German army had permeated every department of German life—all, as he said, through the vigor and skill of Bismarck. He wrote to Juliette to give her his first impression, and he closed, "I shall not take up the political yoke till the fifth or sixth of October. Till then I shall seek adventure, having in my wanderings but a single shadow—my absence from you. I have grown so sweetly habituated to living in your sunlight that I shall walk in gloom until I see you again." These honeyed phrases did not blind Juliette to the stern reality that she and Gambetta were coming to the parting of the ways. She believed he exaggerated the superhuman power of Bismarck. "Gambetta thinks to minimize the cruelty of our reverses by extolling the valor of our conqueror."

Shortly after, Juliette's father died, and Gambetta wrote

her a letter of condolence in which he called her his sister. This letter convinced her—for the time being, at least—of the delicacy and tenderness of his friendship.

Gambetta's public duties had now become so exacting that he could no longer give much time to the management of his newspaper. A popular edition of the République française had been earning money fast and Adam advised Gambetta to sell it before he relinquished his control. Gambetta readily consented and the sale was made. The price was 1,500,000 francs. Adam turned the money over to Gambetta, who was thus enabled to pass the rest of his days without financial troubles. This kindly act had hardly been consummated when Adam died, and Juliette retired to The Briars to wipe away her tears.

When Juliette returned to Paris, she had new cause to realize that Gambetta's heart was not so tender as she had thought. His mother was on the way to Paris, and Gambetta wrote to Juliette not to let the poor old lady stay too long. Juliette felt it her duty to tell her what her son had written. At this disclosure of Gambetta's heartlessness his mother found it hard to check her tears. "I have given up my whole life to him," she murmured, "and now that he has become a great man he casts me aside."

A few days later Juliette was called on to render another service to the man who had been so long her friend. It was brought to her attention that a lady had been seeing one of Gambetta's enemies with an offer to sell him some compromising letters which Gambetta had written her some years before. Juliette sent for Gambetta and told him what she had heard. He was much perturbed, and admitted that he had been on terms of intimacy with the lady, and that she had not only a number of his letters but also a photograph which he had given her and on which he had written some words that would seriously hurt him if they came before the public eye. He begged Juliette to see the lady and use her good offices to hush the matter up. Juliette made an appointment for the lady to come to her house and bring the papers with her. Before they parted Juliette had given the lady six thousand francs and she held in her hands a package containing all the letters and a photograph on which Gambetta had written over his signature the words, "My little queen, I love you more than I love France."

Juliette, at Gambetta's request, had now resumed her regular Friday dinners at which he met the men he felt could be most useful to him in his career. It was nothing but a sense of personal loyalty that induced Juliette to accept this task. With bitter anguish she had abandoned all hope of the "revanche." Gambetta was now talking of disarmament, which filled her with despair. "How," she ejaculated, "can he, our nation's defender, think of disarmament before we have recaptured our Alsace and our Lorraine?" As soon as she could she escaped to The Briars, taking with her the manuscript of three novels, Laïde, Grecque, and Païenne, which were almost ready for publication.

In the course of the winter of 1878, Gambetta paid her another visit—his last visit at The Briars. She had just learned that he had dined with the German ambassador in Paris, and she was so incensed that she could not restrain her indignation. "Who told you that?" Gambetta asked angrily. "I am a Parisian, my dear friend. . . . Don't forget that my husband was prefect of police, and remember there are French spies who watch the spies of Bismarck. . . . The chagrin which your action has caused me made me quit Paris. You are Prussian. I am a Cossack. Our aims are at the opposite poles of French opinion. I have tried to bar your way every time you approached Bismarck."

"You obey your feelings," Gambetta replied, "and I consult my intellect. Very well. Let us follow each our own path."

"My path," she said, "is the national path, laid out by the splendid, proud past of our country; your path is a compromise, a pitfall."

"Well, however we may disagree," replied Gambetta, smiling, "let us keep our friendship untarnished."

"I promise," said Juliette.

That was the end of their intimacy. She continued to see him at her dinners in Paris, but her private interviews with him always ended, as she says, in "scenes." Every now and then he would write her a letter expressing his devotion, and the next time she saw him he would say things that made her boil with indignation. "No friendship in my whole life has contained so great a variety of emotions—worship, admiration, doubt, revolt—as my friendship with Gambetta." After he beca. .e president of the chambre des députés he seemed to her to have cast aside all his patriotic feelings and to be interested only in problems of political strategy. And yet she could never forget that he had always shown a sympathetic understanding of her aspirations and had contributed more than any other man to bringing them to fruition. "For that reason," she says, "nothing ever can or will destroy my affection for him."

During all these years while Juliette was apparently immersed in politics she was devoting a good deal of her leisure time to writing novels. Three of these books—the trilogy which she took with her to The Briars in 1878—were an exposition of her ideas regarding the life of ancient Greece. They were all written in a graceful style, and display considerable imaginative power, but the personages have not sufficient definiteness of character to make the stories particularly interesting. Her best novel, without any question, was her Jean et Pascal, published in 1876. This book illustrates better than any other of her writings Juliette's literary merits and defects. It is a masterpiece of scenic description, and an utterly fantastic portrayal of human emotion. The underlying theme is a frenzied loyalty to France. Pascal, an officer in the army, spurns the love of Madeleine lest it distract him from the service to his country. To show him her indifference, she persuades her brother Jean to take her to Italy where her Italian cousin Spedone is waiting to offer her his hand. Jean, who wants her to marry Pascal, keeps him informed of every fluttering of Madeleine's heart. She tells her brother that she hates Pascal because he has

no other sentiment than affection for his native land. He has
built up an ideal of which he has become the slave, and he
defies any woman to set him free. "Gentleness," the author
comments, "is not inconsistent with courage. The great healer
of man's troubles is woman. To doubt the helpful power of
love is to risk living with a corrupt or ulcered heart." In
the course of time Pascal softens. He writes to Jean that he
had made a mistake in talking to Madeleine of platonic love.
"I was not properly prepared for the perilous voyage of love.
I spent too much time in weighing my baggage." This letter
fell into Madeleine's hands, and it convinced her that he had
really loved her all along.

Madeleine's feelings, of course, had run the whole gamut
before they struck this satisfying chord. The sapphire waters
of Geneva were not enough to soothe her and cause her to lose
her love for the green pastures of dear old France. She
found the spruce trees with their mass of branches clinging
to the earth a poor substitute for the towering oak which
spreads out wider and wider as it reaches the vault of heaven.
In crossing the Alps she gazed with terror across the deep
ravines along which mountain torrents thundered. When
night fell, gorges seemed to rise around her like demons
spreading wide their wings and throwing out long shadows
bathed in mist while the sun lit up the mountain summits
with its expiring flames. "Still higher a deafening voice
roars out above us. A huge cascade leaps in fury from the
entrails of the glacier, falls from a dizzy height with terri-
fying power, and carries along every obstacle in its path until

it reaches a cliff from which it hurls itself into the abyss below and hides itself in a huge cloud of spray."

Not till she gazed upon the picturesque slopes of Italy did her spirits revive. Then she awoke to a new consciousness of the joy of living. The path in front of her seemed all bathed in sunlight and at its end was the promise of a romantic marriage which would enable her to forget the gloom that had settled on her native land. "I am tired of being a patriot," she cries. "I have been forced to shed too many tears over our lost territory. I have lamented too much the loss of our fortresses. I have felt too much chagrin over the ruin of our provinces. I have been driven too violently into national despair. The cup of my suffering has run over, and I am going to turn it upside down. Enough of French tragedy. I shall no more weep for Pascal's Lorraine. I am entering the country where my mother was born. You may cherish, Jean, the image of mutilated France. You are a soldier. You have the right to hate and to dream of vengeance. For myself I want love. I want to dream of youth and happiness. I want smiling fields where there are no wounds. Quitting this gorge inhabited by death I am resolved to live. After all these shadows I need oceans of light."

At Lago Maggiore she breaks into ecstasy over the richness of vegetation. Describing the garden of the Borroméo palace, she says, "Picture a thicket of rose laurel in full bloom. Gray turtle-doves fly above you purling their incantation to Venus. The water of the lake laps and sings against the balustrades of stone. Is it the voices of the nymphs that answer? Never has nature taken more pains or expended more art, or furnished more richness, or given the soil a more luxuriant vegetation to hide the bad taste of man, than it does in the garden of the Borroméos. Eucalyptus, green and black bamboo, tea, camphor, and lemon trees, mimosas, magnolias, green and cork oaks, all sorts of pines, trees from all climates, from every country, from the five parts of the world, caress and embrace one another, and spread with magic power, hiding all kinds of plants too splendid to be so sheltered from public view."

At Lake Como she had her first quarrel with her cousin, who had joined them a few days before. They were sitting under the columns of a ruined sanctuary and Jean was eulogizing nature and the primitive Italian paintings. The love-lorn suitor began to descant upon the early anchorites. "Those men were poets," he declared. "They saw the infinite within themselves." "You believe," she interrupted, "in the poetry of men who detest nature, who find in it only what is rough, hard, intemperate, cruel. You are influenced, my cousin, by the frigid wall of the Church. Your spirit is growing cold. Take care." On his undertaking to show that asceticism was often a revolt against licentiousness, she cried out, "There is no virtue in solitude. It breeds nothing but egotism which gradually undermines the intellect. Selfish contemplation dries up the heart. . . . To be a poet one must love nature. To be virtuous one must respect the principles of social men." She shocked him by her lack of enthusiasm for the Christian faith, but she went on, "I have no faith in Christianity. If you want my frank opinion, woman ought to be an irreconcilable enemy of Christianity. All the distrusts, all the wrongs, all the hatreds of Christian doctrine are directed against her. She is the great peril, the great temptation, the great supporter of Satan. She is the sin, the evil, she and what she inspires—love. Her beauty is a trial, her intelligence a snare, her sensibility a malefactor. The truth is, all the things that men desire, such as generosity, poetry, an artistic nature, are execrable to the believer in Christianity." To further questioning she declared triumphantly that she was a pagan—not a pagan of the days of Pericles, but of the days of Homer, long before Greek civilization began.

In Venice, where her cousin had his palace, and where she had hoped to find the realization of all her poetic fancy, she suffered a rude shock. She had expected a land of mystery, a city, to be sure, of lost power and of crushed pride, but still great in its fall and noble in its tattered emblems, a city with languorous charm, yet beautiful in its decay. Instead, she found a modern city where bustle and excitement jarred upon her nerves and even the gondoliers seemed to have no purpose except to pounce upon her luggage. "But you believe in progress, do you not?" asked her cousin. "Yes, in mechanics, in commerce and industry. I am sensible to progress in ice and fire, in food and locomotives, but I detest it in poetry. In poetry I love what is old and used and faded.

I like the mouldy, the useless, the past. My conception of Venice was poetic, delicate, refined. I do not find it so, and I shall go away."

So her romance was shattered. All the lavish entertainment that her cousin provided wearied her. "All this festivity blinds, it does not attract, me." And her suitor was just a part of what repelled her. "You are a Venetian of Venice," she told him. "You are like your city, a little too modern, a little too handsome, a little too elegant, for me."

Adam's last words to Juliette were an urgent request to continue in the effort to establish the principles of a liberal government for which he had always stood. To follow in his footsteps she required no bidding. In the ten years which they had spent together it would be hard to say which of them had been the vital force. To set up a republic based on universal suffrage had been the central feature of all their thoughts. According to their individual qualifications each had contributed to the cause. Adam's unswerving loyalty to his party, his freedom from personal ambition, his persistency in the face of opposition, had given him a commanding influence in the assemblée. Juliette through her gracious personality had secured the allegiance of a large circle of admirers who gathered around her at the Maison Sallandrouze. After the passing of Adam, in spite of her eagerness to carry out his wishes, she realized that a large part of her influence was gone. To keep his views on governmental questions before the people she needed a wider forum than the social gatherings around her table. Adam had left her an ample heritage and it seemed to her she could use it in no better way than by establishing a new periodical to uphold the republic which her husband had been so instrumental in placing on its feet. She broached the subject to Gambetta and he told her it was folly. "Do you intend in your paper to be as hostile to me personally as you are to my policies?" he asked.

Her answer was: "Since my salon is growing less and less political, I shall naturally not speak much of you. In that way I shall avoid expressing harsh judgments; but, to be perfectly frank, as my pen is to take the place of my tongue, I shall give it freedom. Unable to speak the truth of you in my salon, I shall do so in my review."

"That is almost a declaration of war."

"No, it is a declaration of independence."

The truth is, she was coming more and more to turn for counsel to her literary friends. "My salon is quite changed," she writes a few days later, "but it is no less vital than of old. Conversation has gained in brilliancy what it has lost in weight." It was in these surroundings that her new project found most favor, and as a result La nouvelle revue was founded with a purpose far more literary than political.

George Sand years before had suggested to her that she start a fortnightly publication with the idea of encouraging new writers who were given the cold shoulder by the more conservative journals. Juliette resolved to make that purpose one of the important features in her experiment. It was started with a capital of five hundred thousand francs and among those who joined her in the enterprise were Victor Hugo, Flaubert, Coppée, and Alphonse Daudet. The first number appeared in October, 1879, with a prospectus written by Juliette. Under such auspices it was not strange that the publication was successful almost from the start. More than any other periodical it enabled talented young writers to come before the public. Loti, Bourget, Tinayre, and Anatole France, all made their début in La nouvelle revue. For twenty years after its foundation it occupied Juliette's attention to the exclusion of everything else. She supervised all that appeared in its pages, and many of the articles were from her own pen. From 1885 till 1900 she wrote for each number a résumé of foreign affairs. For a while her hatred of Bismarck was transferred to "perfidious Albion" whose policy, according to her, was to maintain the balance of power by encouraging the continental nations to war against any nation that was becoming formidable.

In the issue of August 1, 1888, she stirred up a hornet's nest by publishing a secret report from Bismarck to his emperor opposing a prospective marriage between the emperor's daughter and Prince Henry of Battenberg. Bismarck denied the authenticity of the report, and in the next issue Juliette published a reply to Bismarck in which she used language that must have caused diplomats to gasp. "The proof of Bismarck's mendacity I have in my possession, and, should I pass away, other arms and other pens will rise to disprove the falsehoods of the most brazen liar of the two worlds." And she closes with these words: "But, lest Bismarck may think he is quite through with me, I promise that the tone of the German press will hereafter dictate my response. Its attacks will provoke counter-attacks from me. To every slur I shall reply by a revelation."

In the issue of September 1st, 1888, she published another letter of Bismarck which she said had been suppressed and which showed that Bismarck was playing politics behind the back of his emperor. This, of course, raised a storm of indignation in Germany. Where she got these letters she did not disclose. The surprising thing is how she dared to attack so vigorously over her own name the most powerful man in Europe.

In 1900 Juliette retired from management of La nouvelle revue and ceased writing articles for its pages. This did not mean that she was anywhere near her end. Nearly twenty years more of life were ahead of her. But she had reached the age when current problems pale into insignificance when confronted with memories of the past. As she looked back over the incidents of a crowded life she was forced to admit that many of her dreams had not come true. Her ambition to attain celebrity as a writer had stopped short of full success. The idea of lifting women to a political equality with men had not entirely prevailed. The hope of recovering the lost provinces had been given up. But the establishment of the French republic, which through all her life had been her most persistent thought, had been triumphantly carried through. Of all these triumphs and disappointments Juliette had a daily record locked up in her safe. She had always been in the habit of keeping a journal in which she jotted down her own impressions and the exact language of the men with whom she talked. To the editing of this journal she devoted the twelve years which followed her withdrawal from La nouvelle revue. As published, it comprised seven volumes, and it proved to be the most valuable of all her literary work.

In one respect these souvenirs stand unique—they were not dressed up to establish the truth or falsity of the writer's views. When they were given to the public Juliette had ceased to be a pagan, she had lost all confidence in Gambetta, she had come to see the folly of attempting to recover Alsace and Lorraine. But she makes no effort to suppress the vehemence of her discarded beliefs. That is the very essence of a diary's worth. To be of service it must reflect contemporary thought. Too often writers of history miss the real significance by giving undue weight to subsequent events. The main consideration is not what ultimately happened, but rather what the forces were by which men's actions were directed.

There are those who carp at Juliette for encumbering the record with recitals of her own emotion. When the Prussian army was at the gates, she braved the perils of a journey to Granville that she might hold her daughter in her arms for one short hour before the siege began. When Gambetta visited her at The Briars she took him out into the fields, where they spent a whole afternoon in search of flowers. When Adam was on his death-bed she kept vigil through day and night until his eyelids closed. Several pages of her diary tell us how her heart vibrated under the influence of these events. Each reader must determine from his own viewpoint whether the record was worth while. But it is this sort of record that reveals the personality of the one who writes. Juliette was a woman for whom sentiment was the most important thing in life. No peril was ever able to shake her love for France. With starvation staring her in the face she continued to denounce as traitors those who counselled peace.

And her courage never left her till the end. The World War found her with unabated determination to resist. All through the darkest days, when German bombs were once more falling on the capital, her country-seat near Paris was again the refuge of men and women who refused to give up hope. Through her efforts a home for permanently disabled French soldiers was established and she was chosen to be its first president. Unhappily she did not survive to witness the ultimate triumph of her cause. But just before her death she was comforted by a touching and well-merited tribute from the front. On the spot where France lost her first victim of the war a gun was set in place and on its pedestal was inscribed the pseudonym of the great patriot, Juliette Lamber.